1891 - F.J.HARPER, Open Math. Scholarship, St.Catherine's College, Cambridge.

1891 - W.TARVER, passed into Sandhurst.

1892 - H.O.PENLEY, History Exhibition, Lincoln College, Oxford.

1892 - O.E.HAYDEN, 2nd Class, Classical Moderations, Ch.Ch.Coll.Oxford.

1892 - W.NELSON, 3rd Class, Natural Science Tripos, Caius College, Cambridge.

1893 - H.S.PRATT, Classical Scholarship, Lincoln College, Oxford.

1893 - W.RICHARDSON, Scholarship at Manitoba University.

1893 - C.RICHARDSON, Scholarship at Manitoba University.

1893 - H.CLEMENTS, Senior Optime, Mathematical Tripos, Cambridge.

1894 - C.B.STRATTON, passed into Woolwich.

1894 - C.K.IRWIN, Trinity College, Dublin, 1st Class in Final Exam., Classical Exhib.

1895 - A.S.HEWITT, Open History Scholarship, Ch.Ch. College, Oxford.

1895 - K.W.BARLEE, Classical Sizarship, Sidney Sussex College, Cambridge.

1895 - H.O.PENLEY, 2nd Class, Final School of History, Lincoln College, Oxford.

1895 - W.V.P.HEXTER, 3rd Class, Final School of History, Exeter College, Oxford.

1895 - H.S.PRATT, 2nd Class, Classical Moderations, Lincoln College, Oxford.

1895 - C.K.IRWIN, Trinity College, Dublin, 2nd Class Honours in Classics.

1895 - H.S.PRATT, 40th place for the Indian Civil Service.

1896 - K.W.BARLEE, Classical Exhibition, Magdalen College, Cambridge.

1896 - H.T.C.WARING, St.Andrew's Univ., Berry Scholarship (£100) in Classics, Campbell Medal. 1st in his year. M.A. with 1st Class Honours in Classics.

1896 - F.S.FINDON, St.Andrew's Univ., Duncan Prize, Miller Prize, and Tullis and Carstairs Medals for Maths.

1897 - F.S.FINDON, St.Andrew's University, M.A., B.Sc., in the shortest time on record.

1898 - W.DAVIS, Mathematical Exhibition, Queen's College, Cambridge.

1898 - H.O.PENLEY, Lothian Prize at Oxford.

1898 - G.E.GORDON, 3rd Class, Classical Moderations.

1898 - K.W.BARLEE, Trinity College, Dublin, 1st Class Hons in Eng.Lit.Classics: Cl.Exhib.

WARWICK SCHOOL
A PORTRAIT

WARWICK SCHOOL
A PORTRAIT

FEATURING PHOTOGRAPHY BY ALAN DAVIDSON

Warwick School: A Portrait

First published in 2014 by Third Millennium Publishing Limited,
a subsidiary of Third Millennium Information Limited.

2–5 Benjamin Street
London
United Kingdom
EC1M 5QL

www.tmiltd.com

ISBN 978 1 908990 14 3

Photography by Alan Davidson
Project Mananagement by Neil Burkey
Designed by Matthew Wilson
Production by Bonnie Murray
Reprographics by Studio Fasoli, Italy
Printed by Printer Trento, Italy

Endpapers: The Honours Boards in
Big School, first painted in 1915.

THIRD MILLENNIUM
PUBLISHING. LONDON

CONTENTS

MICHAELMAS 34

LENT 72

SUMMER 104

FOREWORD

The year 2014 will be marked over the length and breadth of the country, and indeed around the world as one of peerless significance. For Warwick School, the year will be doubly momentous. Not only did Warwickians, staff and old boys alike, play a notable and noble part (as well as paying a terrible price) in the Great War, but we, along with the castle and the town itself, trace our story to a decision made 1,000 years before that tragic war.

Queen Ethelfleda's intention, in the autumn of 914AD, was to create a haven or refuge for her citizens in a land beset by a violence perhaps less familiar to us than the horrors of the Western Front, but every bit as real and destructive for our forerunners. Knowledge of our history since that time is uneven to say the least. Little hard evidence remains even to affirm our existence for many dark centuries, while for others our story can be put together only with much conjecture and assumption. More recent times have, by happy contrast, been painstakingly researched and recorded by our archivists Gervald Frykman and Eric Hadley. Both deserve immense credit for the publication of this book, as does Alison Hartin, whose ambitious vision is realised so magnificenctly here. Contributions

from Old Warwickians, both anecdotes and photographs, have added an invaluable extra dimension to the book and I would like to thank Anne Douglas for her considerable support for this project. This book gives a true flavour of life in our school over many centuries and gives us the chance to celebrate where we have come from, how far we have travelled and, above all, who we are today.

Our story has endured many trials as well as triumphs, twists and turns that are hard to imagine from the relative security, stability and confidence of our current perspective. Over 1,100 years our ability to survive, to look forward, to adapt and to thrive has been peerless. True to our motto, even as we celebrate our past, Warwick School still looks to the future and it is my firm belief that we will continue to provide a haven, a place of both scholarship and fellowship, for pupils, staff and friends of our school over the coming 1,100 years.

Floreat Schola Warwicensis!

Gus Lock
Head Master

A HISTORICAL OVERVIEW

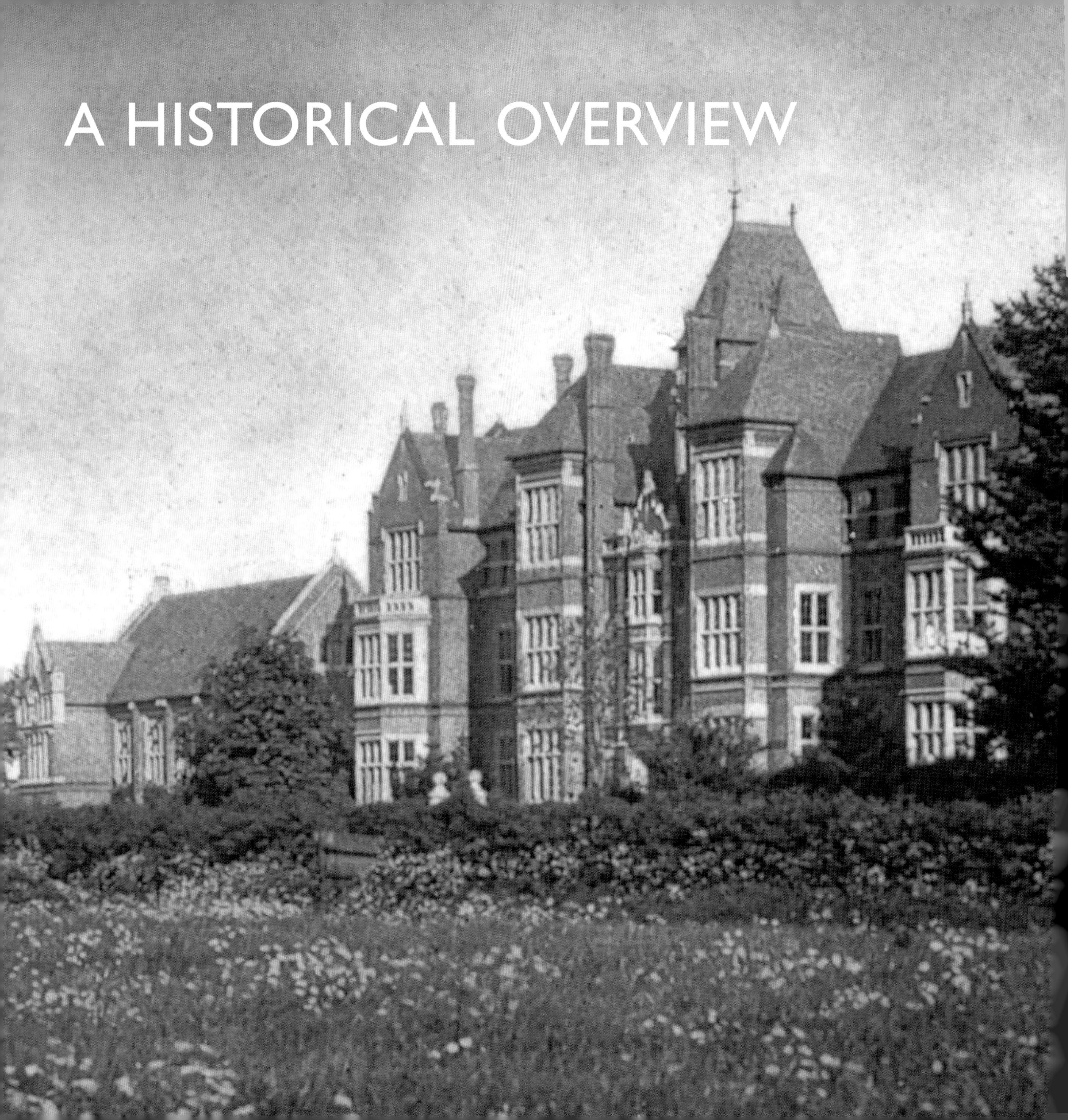

The history of any institution is prone to omission by compression, and that is particularly true when that particular institution has been in existence for 11 centuries, as is the case with Warwick School. It is the purpose of this historical overview, therefore, to shine discrete spotlights on some of the struggles, triumphs and notable persons that play their part in the story of what can claim to be the oldest surviving boys' grammar school in the world.

THE FIRST MILLENNIUM

Warwick School was active in the time of King Edward the Confessor (who reigned from 1042 to 1066), and probably for a century earlier, most likely in the grounds of Warwick Castle. The earliest appearance in history of the town of Warwick itself is in the Anglo-Saxon Chronicle under the year 914, and so for a long time this has been taken as the date for the foundation of Warwick School.

The sole remaining evidence of these earliest years lies in a charter of King Henry I in 1123 merging the school of St Mary's, a newer church, with that of the Church of All Saints, which, it stated, dated from 'tempore Edwardi regis'. Much of the history of this period was wiped out by the Great Fire of Warwick in 1694, including a trove of manuscripts held in St Mary's. We do know that by 1477 lessons were held in the old church of St John the Baptist in the Market Place,

Above: Carved oak statue of Edward the Confessor.

Right: 1610 Speede map of Warwick.

A High Pauement
B Iury Street
C S. Iames Chappel
D West Street
E Quene Well street
F Lothenhull Lane
G Sakteforde
H Hodg forde
I Wal ditche
K Powke lane
L Dogge Lane
M St Peters Chapel
N Smiths Street
O Coten ende
P S. Nicholas church
Q St Nicholas Street
R Goal hall Lane
S Vineyard Lane
T St Maryes Church
V Churche street
W Cannon Rowe
X Northgate street
Y Pibble Lane
Z Both hall
3 St Iohns church
4 Rother Chipping
5 Horse Chipping
6 Swane Lane
7 Castle strete
8 Brittaine Lane
9 Walkers Lane
10 Mill street
11 Warytree street
12 Crosse streat
13 Shire Hall.
14

and the school was still there when King Henry VIII re-founded it as 'The King's New Scole of Warwyke' in 1545. At this point the new grammar school moved to what is now the Lord Leycester Hospital, and later on to St Peter's Chapel over the Eastgate, which is now part of King's High School for Girls.

It is not yet known where the school was in the 17th century, but there were a few notable school masters during that time, including the epigrammatist John Owen (school master c.1560–c.1614). (An example of his work being, in a translation from the original Latin: 'I do not know, or if I do know, I do not know that I know, and in the Socratic fashion I know that I know nothing.') Another prominent master of the 17th century was Revd Thomas DuGard (school master 1633–49), later Rector of Barford Church, who did so much to record the history and daily life of the school in his Latin diary, which still awaits a full translation.

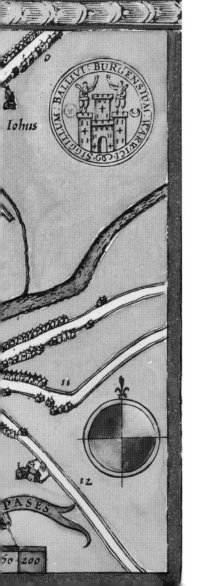

THE MOVE TO ST MARY'S

The grammar school moved to the disused medieval buildings of the Vicars Choral in St Mary's churchyard around 1697, and stayed there for the next 200 years. The school's progress (or lack thereof, as the case may have sometimes been) in the 18th century was overseen by the long tenures of three men: Richard Lydiate from 1701 until his death in 1730; his son Francis 1730 until 1769; and, from 1769 until 1791, the Revd James Roberts, whose tenure was by most accounts disastrous.

Despite initially thriving, with up to 60 boarders at one point, by the end of the 1700s 'there were no boarders and very few, if any, free scholars'. The year 1792 saw the start of Revd George Innes's 50-year mastership, and the school's fortunes once again fluctuated wildly. Although Innes revived the almost completely depleted student body, many pupils during his time received no more than what would today be considered tutorials, with most of the subjects being taught by other local schools. Educational reforms and the shake-up of local charities dramatically improved the school after Innes's death, leading to the introduction of a modern curriculum under new Headmaster Revd Herbert Hill (1843–76).

A proper teaching staff was employed and a bed was provided for every boy for the first time. Difficult as it might be to believe today, it was only in 1871 that a list of students attending the school (numbering about 50 at that time) began to be kept. In the 1870s three new schools were proposed, and all of them had begun operations by 1879: the King's Grammar School, on a new site south of the River Avon, which featured a Classical curriculum; the King's Middle School in The Butts, which provided a 'commercial education' for 'less academic' boys; and the King's High School for Girls, in Landor House, Smith Street.

Above: School room in St Mary's churchyard, 1870.

Right: St Mary's Hall, seen here in the 1920s.

Above: Whole-school photograph, c.1876.

Right: Revd G. Innes (Headmaster, 1792–1842).

Far right: Revd H. Hill (Headmaster, 1843–76).

A NEW SITE AND A NEW NAME

The late Victorian era was initially one of success and growth, showing no signs of trouble brewing. The first Headmaster in Warwick School's present site was Revd William Fisher MacMichael, who started at the school in 1876 and was present at the opening of the new school buildings, designed by John Cundall and costing £12,300, plus £1,500 for the Chapel, on 1 August 1879. The only items taken from the school's previous site at St Mary's were oak beams for use in the construction of the Headmaster's pig sty,

although a bell from the Eastgate Chapel dating from 1730 was installed in the tower, where it remains to this day.

The old school buildings were sold and demolished a year later, leaving only the gateway, steps and outer wall of the schoolyard. An official set of School Rules were drawn up by the next Headmaster, Revd William Grundy. (Rule number two was 'No boy may either use or possess a catapult. Pistols, cannons, and fire-arms of every sort are prohibited.') On the new site a Junior Department (now

The earliest surviving photograph of the back of the school, 1897.

the Junior School) was opened in 1889 and a Chemistry laboratory was constructed which much later would become the school museum. The number of pupils had risen to 135 in 1885 (with six staff), and reached 168 ten years later.

There were developments in the school's legacy also, the most significant of which was the introduction of a new (and at the time unofficial) name – Warwick School, coined by Revd John Pearce Way, early in his headmastership. He can also be credited with the motto *Altiora Peto*, which translates to 'I aim for higher things'. An English-language School Song was written, called 'Here's a Song for All'. The Cadet Corps was established by Colonel Cooke, a local soldier and last surviving pupil of Revd Innes, and The Limes were planted. The first edition of *The Portcullis* was published and Oxford Scholarships began to be won by Warwickian pupils.

KING'S GRAMMAR SCHOOL, WARWICK.
RULES. *as issued by W.G.*

1.—Either College caps or hats with the School ribbon are to be worn outside the School. Hats with the School ribbon are preferable on week-days, but College caps should be worn on Sunday. Blue caps may be worn inside the School gates except on Sunday.

2.—No boy may either use or possess a Catapult. Pistols, Cannons, and fire-arms of every sort are prohibited.

3.—Stone throwing and dirt throwing of every description is prohibited.

4.—During School hours there must be no shouting, whistling, noise or disorder, in any portion of the School buildings.

5.—Neither desks nor doors are to be slammed.

6.—Day boys may go upstairs for any purpose directly connected with their work; otherwise, the whole building above the ground floor, including the staircase, is out of bounds

Boarders are requested to take notice of the following RULES *in addition to those which apply to Day boys as well as to themselves.*

1.—On Week-day mornings the Dormitories are closed at 8, on Sundays at 8.30. They are opened in the evening at 9. On half-holidays they are open for half-an-hour after dinner; also on half-holidays during the Cricket season from 6 to 6.30 p.m., and during the Football season from 4.30 to 5 p.m. The wardrobe keeper will attend after dinner on half-holidays to give out clothing, and will open the Dormitories in succession on other days for the same purpose and at the same time. On all other occasions, except those specified above, admission to the Dormitories must be obtained by application to the matron.

2.—Clean linen will be given out to all boys twice a week, but collars and handkerchiefs can be obtained from the wardrobe keeper any day after dinner, unless she sees reason to refuse. No collar or handkerchief will be given out on such occasions unless the one in use is returned. Boys who have got their feet wet are to make immediate application to the matron or wardrobe keeper for a change, without waiting till the usual time.

3.—After games, and in the evening, boys must change their boots for house shoes before entering the Dormitories.

CRISIS, AND THE VICTORIAN LEGACY

The ten years from 1896 – under Headmaster Revd Robert Percival Brown until 1903 and Revd William Theodore Keeling thereafter – were ones of increasing crisis for the school. They culminated in its economic collapse and temporary closure, the flight of Headmaster Keeling, the sacking of all the staff, the withdrawal of most of the boys and a merger with the King's Middle School in 1906. As one might expect with an institution that has survived as long as Warwick School, even during this dark decade there were more than a few positive achievements. Not least of these were improvements to the estate.

The school chapel was completed (apart from the gallery), including a perpendicular new wing, and Keeling supervised the installation of a stained-glass window in the east window of the chancel. A Science block was constructed (which is known to current students as the Music block) and the dining room gained its wooden panelling. Changes went beyond bricks and mortar too, extending to the implementation of the House system and the composition of a second School Song, in Latin: 'Floreat Domus',

which means, 'May This House Flourish'. 'Floreat Domus' was written for the lavish festival known as the Warwick Pageant which took place in 1906, at the height of the school's crisis.

There were major movements towards giving the past its proper due, as well, with the formation of the Old Warwickian Association (or 'Club', as it was first known) in 1898 'to unite OWs in perpetual fraternity on the basis of loyal devotion to the school'. Life membership was set at £1 10s and its first dinner was held in Holborn in London. The driving force behind the Club was Norman W. Brown, whose name is engraved in one of the panels of the school chapel. Of equal importance was the publication of *History of Warwick School*, the school's first, written by A.F. Leach between 1894 and 1906.

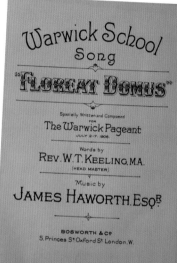

Left: A.F. Leach's History of Warwick School.

Left: The Chapel in 1903.

Below: 1906 pageant at Warwick Castle.

Left: King's Middle School, 1902.

Below: Revd W.T. Keeling (Headmaster, 1903–06).

Bottom: Revd R.P. Brown (Headmaster, 1896–1902).

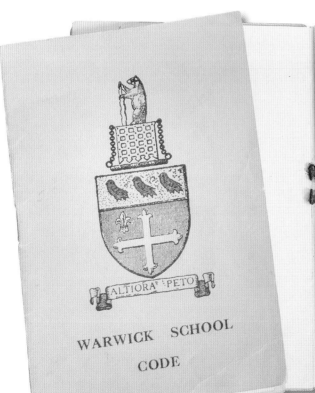

WARWICK SCHOOL CODE

WARWICK SCHOOL CODE

I.—GENERAL.

1.—BEHAVIOUR. Behave well, but naturally. Walk briskly, don't slouch, don't eat in the streets. Take trouble to speak well, and be courteous. On the pavement, give the inside to women and children.

2.—DRESS. Dress smartly, wearing regulation School clothes and cap (not at an angle) to and from School. Be well groomed, with hair short and well brushed, neat nails, shoes shining and in good condition, and clothes well brushed and without stains, tears or missing buttons.

3.—CAPPING. Cap properly visitors (use discretion), masters and other Warwickians if they are with adults. (You should be capped back). When in uniform, salute, or if you are on a bike, give "eyes right (or left)".

4.—Firearms and catapults are forbidden. Never throw things.

5.—Smoking, swearing, drinking, and vulgar conversation are forbidden.

6.—Senior boys should feel a certain sense of responsibility in any group of boys in or out of School.

AFTER THE FIRST THOUSAND YEARS

The long-overdue setting down of the school's history proved to be prescient, as the 20th century was to be a time of profound transformation, during which many of the attributes that define Warwick School for today's students would be established. One of these being the statue of Edward the Confessor, purchased by the Old Warwickian Association at just under £40 in 1924, which graces the main entrance. After the enormous turmoil of the accession of the new Headmaster physicist H.S. Pyne, the school grew rapidly in numbers, but this growth of course came only after the devastation of the First World War, which claimed 88 Old Warwickians and two former staff.

This growth is evidenced by the earliest-surviving whole-school photograph, taken in 1920. By the late 1920s, there were almost 400 boys in the school, including 146 (very profitable) boarders, almost double the permitted number, and the staff had grown to 25 at this time as well. In order to accommodate the needs of this expanding student body, by 1920 New Buildings were built, as was the engineering shop (which is still used today for the same purpose) and an outdoor swimming pool, no doubt welcomed by all. The 1920s also saw the first use of electric lighting in the school, replacing the former gas fixtures.

There were changes in extra curricular activities, such as the joint debates held with King's High School and the first of what were to be many future Science Exhibitions. A long association with music was strengthened with the creation of a school orchestra and the introduction of the annual carol service held in St Mary's Church. The school's inextricable links to the community were shown by the initiation of a programme which allowed for eight free places to be offered to local elementary school pupils and the first of what was to become an annual visit by the Town Crier, soon to be one of the school's most recognisable traditions.

H.S. Pyne (Headmaster, 1906–28) with staff in 1927.

Front View, Main Building, Warwick School.

Left: The front of the school, c.1920.

Below: Second Master and Bursar M.M. Clark, who worked at Warwick School from 1899 to 1949.

Right: The tragic 1st XV of 1912–13, of whom nine lost their lives in the First World War.

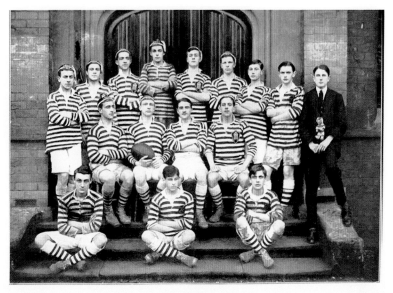

ÆC NEILLE. PHOTO.   WARWICK.

Warwick School Football Team, 1912–13.

J. Wood.   H. J. Smith.   H. V. O. Robinson.   C. G. Dixon.   L. J. C. Seaman.   G. H. Abbott.   A. H. Dawkes.   C. R. W. Lamplough.   G. H. Walker. (Touch-Judge.)
R. G. Hart.   G. W. Mann, Capt.   C. T. Coyne.   R. F. Jardine.
A. S. Garrett.   E. W. [1912-13 1ST XV]   E. L. Ward.

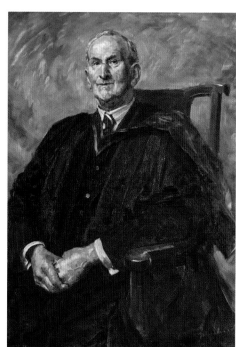

19

EARLY 20TH CENTURY GROWTH

The First World War, having claimed the life of his son Eric, had a particularly shattering effect on Headmaster H.S. Pyne, and in commemoration of his loss he generously paid for the Chapel gallery and west window as a war memorial. Despite this addition, however, and along with a new stage constructed in Big School, on the whole the school was becoming somewhat run down by the late 1920s. The incoming Headmaster in 1928, the linguist G.A. Riding from Rugby School, saw himself as a 'new broom sweeping clean'.

Riding's reign was not without discord, as for example when, early on in his headmastership, he removed the boarding cubicles and replaced them with large, military-style, open dormitories – a move not popular with the boys, who no doubt mourned their lost privacy. His tenure was blighted in particular by a fire in 1930 purposely set by a student in the Elstow dormitory wing. Riding was determined, however, and his era saw many advances, including the design of the school badge and the school uniform, both of which are still in use to this day. It also saw the start of overseas school trips and (less happily) Form Orders, which entailed the boy at the bottom of the list being flogged in front of the whole school.

Under Riding, Music and Drama flourished as never before. It was Riding who started the tradition (lasting until the 1980s) of Gilbert and Sullivan performances, and in 1928 the new stage in Big School featured one of its first plays, Shakespeare's *Julius Caesar*. The sport of boxing reached its peak of prominence in the 1930s. After Riding left in 1933 he was replaced by the school's shortest-serving modern Headmaster, Eric Percival Smith, known for the previously unheard-of habit of calling boys by their first name. Politics thrived during his short term, with the most popular school society being the League of Nations Union, and Percival Smith also started production of the Blue Book, the publication of which continues to this day.

Below: The first Blue Book, 1934.

Below left: Big School, c.1920, with new interior decoration including Honours Boards.

WARWICK SCHOOL.
(Chartered by Edward the Confessor)

ALTIORA PETO

September 20th, 1934.

Above: A production of King John, 1926.

Below: E.P. Smith (Headmaster, 1933–36).

Above: G.A. Riding (Headmaster, 1928–33).

Right: The west window of the Chapel, donated by H.S. Pyne, 1925.

THE SECOND WORLD WAR

The long headmastership of the Cornish chemist Arthur Henry Burdick Bishop (1936–62) got off to a rocky start, when he decided to re-open the Junior House – which had been closed in 1935 by agreement with a local preparatory school – as a private junior school in 1938. This led to his temporary suspension from the Headmasters' Conference, in turn instigating him to begin a vigorous campaign which included writing to the most famous Old Warwickians of the time, most notably the Poet Laureate John Masefield, in order to get himself reinstated.

Bishop encountered further legal problems when he was sued for damages in 1941 at Birmingham Assizes. A 14-year-old boarder doing unsupervised wartime agricultural work in the summer of 1940 at Charlecote lost an eye when a clod of earth was thrown at him. There were, of course, even larger things to worry about. As in the conflict of 1914–18, the number of pupils in the school actually grew during the Second World War, the total rising to 450 by 1946. It proved difficult to appoint and retain adequate staff, and the school was forced to share its premises with an evacuated Birmingham School between 1939 and 1940. Air-raid shelters were dug, gas-masks were assembled, and wartime losses of Old Warwickians were heavy.

The most fundamental change at this time, however, occurred as a result of the 1944 Butler Education Act, one aim of which was to make secondary education free of charge for all pupils. At Warwick the fees had to more than triple (to £16 per term for day-boys), as the substantial Local Education Authority (LEA) subsidy to the school was due to come to an end. The LEA did still provide complete funding for 45 'free place' boys in every year, and also institute a fees remission scheme for parents earning less than £7 10s per week.

Above: *Return from CCF camp, 1940.*

Below: *The Second World War memorial in the Chapel.*

Jam was on ration. We could bring our own eggs (one egg a term was supplied by the kitchen). You would put your name on your own egg. We used to bring our own baked beans to supplement Sunday tea. The beans were cold although we did try warming them on the 'hot' water pipes.

— John Cooper, WS 1940–49

GREATER LOVE HATH NO MAN THAN THIS

1939

IN GLORIOUS MEMORY
OF OLD WARWICKIANS

WHO GAVE THEIR LIVES IN
THE SECOND WORLD WAR

ALTIORA PETO

1945

T. F. ADAMS			J. B. COLEMAN
R. ADAMS			G. F. MEASURES
J. R. ALDIS			H. T. MEASURES
D. J. ANDREWS			M. J. PEASE
J. B. BEESTON-BANCROFT	J. DAVIES	J. H. HUNT	J. RANDALL
G. L. BENTLEY	R. E. DAVIES	J. K. CHARLES JONES	R. F. REDLEY
B. BISHOP	R. W. DAVIS	P. JOYNSON	D. P. W. ROWAN-ROBINSON
R. BRADBURY	C. FALKINER	R. R. LEAN	G. M. SCHOOLEY
H. B. BURN	M. FANTHAM	P. J. LEES	A. H. SPARROW
L. G. BURTON	F. D. FARMAN	J. LEWIS	P. G. TEALL
R. T. CHAMBERS	D. A. GREEN	E. F. LINES	R. THACKER
J. H. COLBOURNE	A. E. GREEN	P. LONDON	R. E. THORNLEY
R. T. COLLIER	P. W. GOODWIN	E. E. MANISON	H. G. TINGLE
F. H. CONSTABLE	F. J. HEGAN	R. F. MARRACK	T. E. WESSON
W. B. S. CUNYNGHAME	L. CARDWELL HILL	M. C. MATTINSON	J. de BURGH WHITE
E. W. DAVEY	R. G. HORNE	W. L. McKENZIE	L. SHINER
F. N. S. COWIE	J. PROSSER	V. H. C. MITCHELL	J. LATIMER

INDEPENDENCE AND POST-WAR STABILITY

In 1946 the governors were forced to declare that Warwick School would need to become independent, signalling a new direction for the school. Although there were many improvements at the close of the 1940s, such as the asphalting of the area under The Limes up to the Junior House and the construction of the Orlits buildings in the Biological Garden, student numbers had at that point nearly doubled in size over 15 years without much growth of its estate. This issue was addressed in the 1950s with the help of a Memorial Endowment Fund, starting with a new Biology laboratory and the Memorial Gymnasium. New Chemistry and Physics laboratories were also built, leaving Keeling's original science block to be taken over by the Geography and History departments.

There were changes to education itself at this time, as the School Certificate examinations were replaced by O and A levels – a move not welcomed by Bishop, thinking that the new style of teaching favoured breadth of knowledge over depth. It was a success nonetheless, and by 1957 the A level pass rate at the school was 95 per cent. Sports thrived in this era as well, with significant victories and advances in cricket, tennis, athletics, water polo and the school's prime sport, rugby. The CCF began to venture further afield, with trips to France, Belgium, Italy and Austria.

The 1950s were also to feature visits by distinguished persons, such as Viscount Montgomery of Alamein and Sir Anthony Eden, Prime Minister 1955–57, whose sister, the Countess of Warwick, chaired the school's governing body in the 1930s. These were followed by a highly successful visit by Her Majesty The Queen Mother in 1958.

Thanks to his strong leadership, after two and a half tempestuous decades at the helm, A.H.B. Bishop was ready to hand over a now-thriving Warwick School. By the time he retired in 1962, there were 742 pupils and 44 staff in the senior and junior schools.

At that time the school's central heating system was solid fuel fired. This meant that significant piles of coke were to be found in various places around the school estate. A simple fact of life to us all, but it became a source of anxiety to those planning the route of Her Majesty, Queen Elizabeth The Queen Mother, as she toured the school in the autumn of 1958.

The simple solution was to have rows of boys standing on benches to block such offensive views. However, no account had been taken of the curiosity of the Queen Mother: 'Why are those boys standing on benches?' she asked of the Headmaster. 'They are hiding a dreadful sight, Ma'am' was Mr Bishop's reply.

When a little further on she came across the next tier of boys, she wasted no time with questions. 'Another dreadful sight, Headmaster?!' The story became a favourite of Mr Bishop's, so much so that over 40 years later, when I met his son, Andrew, he said that no family occasion had passed without the story being retold.

— **Paul Ramage**, WS 1948–59

Left: Headmaster A.H.B. Bishop welcomes The Queen Mother to the school in 1958.

Below: Buglers announce the Queen's Accession, 1952.

Right: P. Whitlam hoists a flag for the Coronation, 1953.

GROWTH

The historian Patrick William Martin, Headmaster, 1962–77, continued the path of success set down by those who came before him. Martin's headmastership also brought about countless changes to the school structures, with the English and Mathematics departments getting new teaching blocks and Big School being converted into the school library. The Guy Nelson Hall was completed in 1969, and Bridge House was purchased, along with its land, to house the Art Department. The New Buildings, always intended to be temporary, were finally demolished after 55 years usage and, perhaps most memorably of all, the school bought its first blue and white minibus.

The wider community continued to play a large role in school life, with the introduction of parents' evenings, the establishment of the Friends of Warwick School and implementation of a Community Service Organisation, which operated on a much wider scale than previously with boys going out into the community for charitable

and voluntary work. The compulsory wearing of the school cap was abolished, and the school's first computer was built (even if a modern audience might not recognise it as such!). In response to parallel changes on a national level, the School Mathematics Project, the Cambridge Classics Project and Nuffield Science were brought in, and the school's first language laboratory was created.

Improvements such as these meant that more and more students were proceeding on to higher education. The new Music School built in 1965 (now part of the Staff Common Room) brought with it a rise in both the number of and participation in cultural events, with musicals, plays and summer concerts aplenty. School societies did well in the 1960s and 1970s, though some, such as the Folk Music Club, lasted little longer than the era itself. With all of the radical shifts in society at large, Warwick School continued to grow, Headmaster Martin keeping sage control all the while, until he stepped down from his post in 1977.

Below left: Pat Martin, Headmaster (1962–77).

Below: School bus, 1971.

Right: Guy Nelson Hall.

The fire brigade was a splendid thing to volunteer for as it gave one the opportunity to play around with a lot of water in the middle of the night. Fire practices were in the day and at night. It was always imagined that the roof of 'Big School' had caught fire. The intrepid personnel would fit the standpipe, connect the hoses and nozzles and, at least once, squirt the water up the roof plane so that it got under the tiles and into the hall.

— Anon

Above: School fire brigade, 1966.

Left: The Orlits, 1973.

27

MODERNISATION

Innovation rolled on and political events, over which he had no control, soon forced mathematician and Olympic hockey player J.A. Strover (Headmaster, 1977–88) to consider a number of radical changes. One of these was the alteration of the intake, as the Assisted Places Scheme replaced the Local Education Authority's arrangement of paying for free places. In two moves that would have been cheered by the schoolchildren of the day, corporal punishment was totally abolished in the school, as were Saturday morning classes, in 1982. The number of reports on boys by staff was increased, and staff themselves started to be appraised around the same time.

O level and CSE examinations were replaced by GCSEs in 1988, and an A level pass rate of 90 per cent was achieved. Craft, Design and Technology became an academic subject. The school's first dedicated computer room opened in 1981, with half a dozen Commodore PETs, and was soon to be replaced in 1986 by a full-size room with 17 BBC micros. Computing became an academic subject shortly thereafter. The school gained its first English block, followed by the creation of a Sixth Form Centre in the main building.

Enoch Powell gave a defence of the Classics at the 1984 Speech Day despite the protestors gathered on Myton Road. The Junior School had a science laboratory installed and new facilities for Art and Music. A move in the early 1980s to shut down the boarding houses was quashed, and they were instead completely refurbished. The number of boarders during this time averaged 55, with an increase in pupils from Hong Kong. Sport continued to prosper through this period, members of the Sailing Club participated in a Tall Ships Race, and the rugby team completed a tour of Zimbabwe in 1985.

All told, Strover's vision for Warwick School was happily achieved.

Left: Prospectus shot, 1970s.

Below: The school seen from the air, 1970s.

Left: 1986 CCF Adventurous Training.

Above: First desktop computer, 1981.

Left: A game of pool in the cellars.

Below: J.A. Strover (Headmaster, 1977–88).

TOWARDS THE NEW MILLENNIUM

Physicist Dr Philip James Cheshire (Headmaster, 1988–2002), saw to it that the facilities of virtually every department in the school were improved. Amongst the multitude of refurbishments, the 1949 Orlits building was replaced by a purpose-built Geography and History block, with Lady Antonia Fraser attending the 1996 official opening. The Music Department moved into Keeling's gutted 1905 Science laboratories, making huge gains in practice and performance space. The 1911 outdoor swimming pool was finally filled in, and was replaced by a new Sports Hall, while the 1890 gymnasium was converted into a Sixth Form Centre.

The Library and IT department were moved to a new building named after Old Warwickian John Masefield and a new organ was built for the Chapel in 1992 as a result of the generosity of Ralph Thornton. The old library became an extension dining room and functions area which came to be known as the Pyne Room, and all staff were issued with laptop computers. A drama studio was built at the back of the Guy Nelson Hall and a brand new theatre was constructed on the site of (and named after) Bridge House. An Astroturf games pitch was installed and the entire Junior School was refurbished and extended into a quadrangle.

In a step that further secured the safety of the heritage of a venerable institution, the school's first Archivist, Gervald Frykman, was appointed. Top GCSE grades at the school increased from 33 per cent at the start of Cheshire's headmastership to 59 per cent at the end. Guests of the school in these years included Sir Ben Kingsley, Dame Judi Dench and the politician-turned-novelist Ann Widdecombe. Drama, Sport and the CCF moved forward in leaps and bounds. The Towards 2000 Appeal was instrumental in fundraising for the building campaign and collaboration with the sister school, King's High School, developed during this time.

Below: Opening of the new swimming pool, 1992.

Bottom: Bridge House Theatre, opened in 2000.

Science experiments, 1990s.

Left: The Junior School which was rebuilt and extended during 2001–2.

Far left: Using a metalwork lathe.

Below left: Creative work in the Art department.

Below: Dr P.J. Cheshire (Headmaster, 1988–2002).

THE 21ST CENTURY

The recent developments at Warwick School have been among the most financially ambitious in the school's history. Edward Halse joined the school as Head Master in August 2002 and brought with him a commitment to develop the caring nature of the institution and the role of information technology in teaching and administration. Interactive whiteboards sprang up around the school, and all staff were encouraged to become computer literate, possibly in an attempt to ensure that their ICT awareness kept up with that of the younger generation!

The school experienced during this era a continuing programme of major building development. In addition to the Junior School extension which opened in 2002, dramatic changes came with the building of a £6.1 million state-of-the-art Science Centre, named after Dr Cheshire, which opened in 2007. In 2008, the previous Science and Mathematics blocks were replaced by a three-storey building, named after former master Ralph Thornton, dedicated to the teaching of Mathematics, Classics and Religion and Philosophy, the latter subject being the last to be moved out of the 1879 main school building. It became clear that the Sports Centre needed to be extended and in 2013 additional facilities for changing, teaching academic PE and a modern pavilion, named after Ed Halse, were opened by Lord Coe.

Collaboration between the three schools in the Foundation also became a key feature of everyday life at the school. Sixth Form girls from King's High School joined the Warwick School CCF, some joint teaching started in the Sixth Form and joint drama productions and music concerts are a regular feature in the calendar. The school has, arguably, never offered a wider opportunity for boys to develop their artistic, dramatic, musical and design skills. Musicians continue to make a name for

An aerial view of the school, 2013.

Left: Warwick Town Remembrance Parade, 2006.

Below: E.B. Halse (Headmaster, 2002–13).

Above: Cheshire Science Centre, officially opened in June 2008.

Below: The 2007 Daily Mail Cup. Warwick School won the U18 rugby title for the first time in the school's history.

themselves whilst the number of boys taking lessons and the number of music bands and groups has never been so high. In Drama some significant cultural achievements have been seen with plays and musicals, classical and modern being performed.

Sport has always been a central feature of the school's provision and the current century has seen more sports played and national standards achieved in many of them. The school won the Daily Mail Cup for the first time in its history in 2007 and then again in 2013, and took the National Water Polo title in 2006. Warwick School

also has an outstanding record in Channel Swimming, with successful cross-Channel Swims completed in 2006, 2009 and 2012.

Edward Halse presided over a strengthening of the school's reputation in so many respects, including the best academic performance to date. He could feel certain that his vision for the school was being fulfilled when he retired in August 2013. His successor, Augustus Lock (known to all as Gus), joined Warwick from Merchant Taylor's School in Northwood. His first year as Head Master marks the prestigious 1,100th anniversary of this remarkable school.

MICHAELMAS

MICHAELMAS

September marks the start of a new term and for many the start of their school career at Warwick School. The new boys arrive in their new, often over-sized blazers, apprehensive about the day, week or even years ahead of them.

The staff meeting at the start of the Michaelmas term usually includes mention of the School Roll. Records indicate that school numbers dropped to 28, including one boarder, in 1868. In September 2013, at the start of his first term as Head Master, Gus Lock announced a School Roll of 1,214. Staff now number over 320, more than the number of pupils at the school for the first 900 years.

This increase in numbers is most apparent in school assembly, where boys now spill out of the Guy Nelson Hall. The move to the Guy Nelson Hall in 1970 was necessary after the school outgrew its previous venue for assemblies in 'Big School' now the Pyne Room.

Boarders arrive the day before the start of term. Arriving from Heathrow after a flight from Hong Kong contrasts greatly with the arrival of boys in the 19th and 20th centuries, when many boarders were from the local area. Boarders made up a far bigger proportion of the school in earlier years but overall numbers have remained fairly consistent since the late 19th century. In 1843 the school re-introduced boarding and, for the first time, a bed was provided for each boy!

The Town Crier makes his annual visit before the Michaelmas half term, as he has done since 1912. Traditionally, the Town Crier requests the Head Master to grant permission for an extra week's holiday at half term for the boys.

Remembrance Day is respectfully acknowledged at Warwick School by the CCF and in Chapel. The CCF take part in the Town's Remembrance Parade and the CSM places a wreath at the town's memorial near St Mary's Church.

The Chapel Service on Remembrance Sunday honours all Warwickians who lost their lives in active service, in and since the two World Wars. On November 11th each year, from the chapel altar, Headmaster H.S. Pyne would read out the names of the 90 Old Warwickians, including two staff, who fell in the First World War. In current times the Sunday service remembers those who died in both World Wars as well as in recent conflicts.

Whilst drama and music performances now take place throughout the year, the autumn months see the first big drama production of the year. In contrast to early performances at Warwick School, the female parts are now played by girls from King's High School. In recent years, high-profile drama and music productions have included Les Misérables and Hamlet.

The Thornton Building, completed in 2008.

Left: Setting up for school assembly in Guy Nelson Hall.

Below: Harvest Festival, 1976.

The tradition of performing Gilbert and Sullivan Operas started in the 1930s and continued until the mid 1980s.

Music has come a long way at Warwick School since 1881 when the Prospectus, held in the County Record Office, shows that there was a teaching staff of three (plus the Headmaster) who taught all the classics in the school and the 'Drawing Masters', together with a local organist who taught 'Vocal Music'. Warwick School Orchestra's inaugural concert was in December 1915. The orchestra consisted of five violins, a cello, a piccolo, a piano and two drums – but it was a start!

There are now over 70 different choral, orchestral and music groups and bands who rehearse and perform regularly.

In 1848, 'small games' were played at the school: football and cricket on Saltisford Common. In 1927 'Rugger' was timetabled for Wednesday and Saturday afternoons. It had been thought that hockey was a relatively late innovation at Warwick School; however,

Above: Carol Service at St Mary's, 2013

there is reference to the hockey season in John Pearce Way's Master's Book in 1889. It probably wasn't until the late 1960s that hockey was established alongside rugby with competitive fixtures and games sessions.

The term ends with Christmas celebrations, most significantly the carol service at St Mary's Church. It is likely the annual walk up to St Mary's derived from the parade to the Church in 1912, for a service 'to perpetuate and revive the bond of connection between the two institutions'.

The school has always had strong links with the church ever since its foundation under the tutelage of All Saints' Church. The re-foundation of the school in 1545, as the King's New School of Warwick, decreed that the schoolmaster was to be appointed by the crown and that he and the vicar of St Mary's should live in the same house! Between c.1697 and 1879, the school was run in the old College of the Vicars Choral in St Mary's churchyard.

Christmas celebrations are probably most evident in the Junior School, where Christmas hats are accepted attire and the Junior School concert fills the Guy Nelson Hall with festive cheer. The Christmas 'stagger' is a relatively new event in the Junior School and involves the boys running around the school fields before exchanging Christmas gifts.

The Christmas Day Chapel Service is always a popular service for boys, their families, OWs and the whole school community.

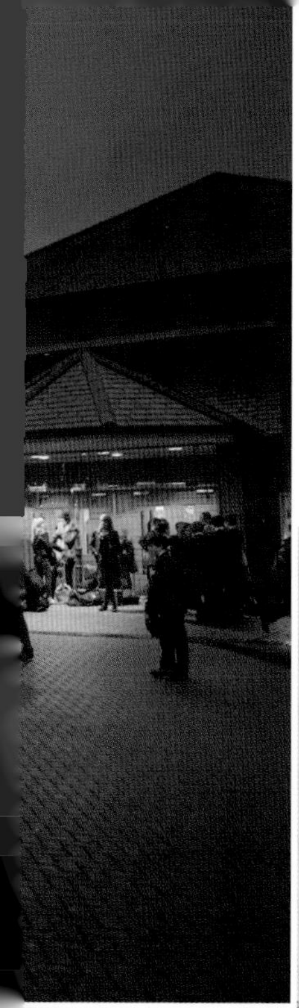

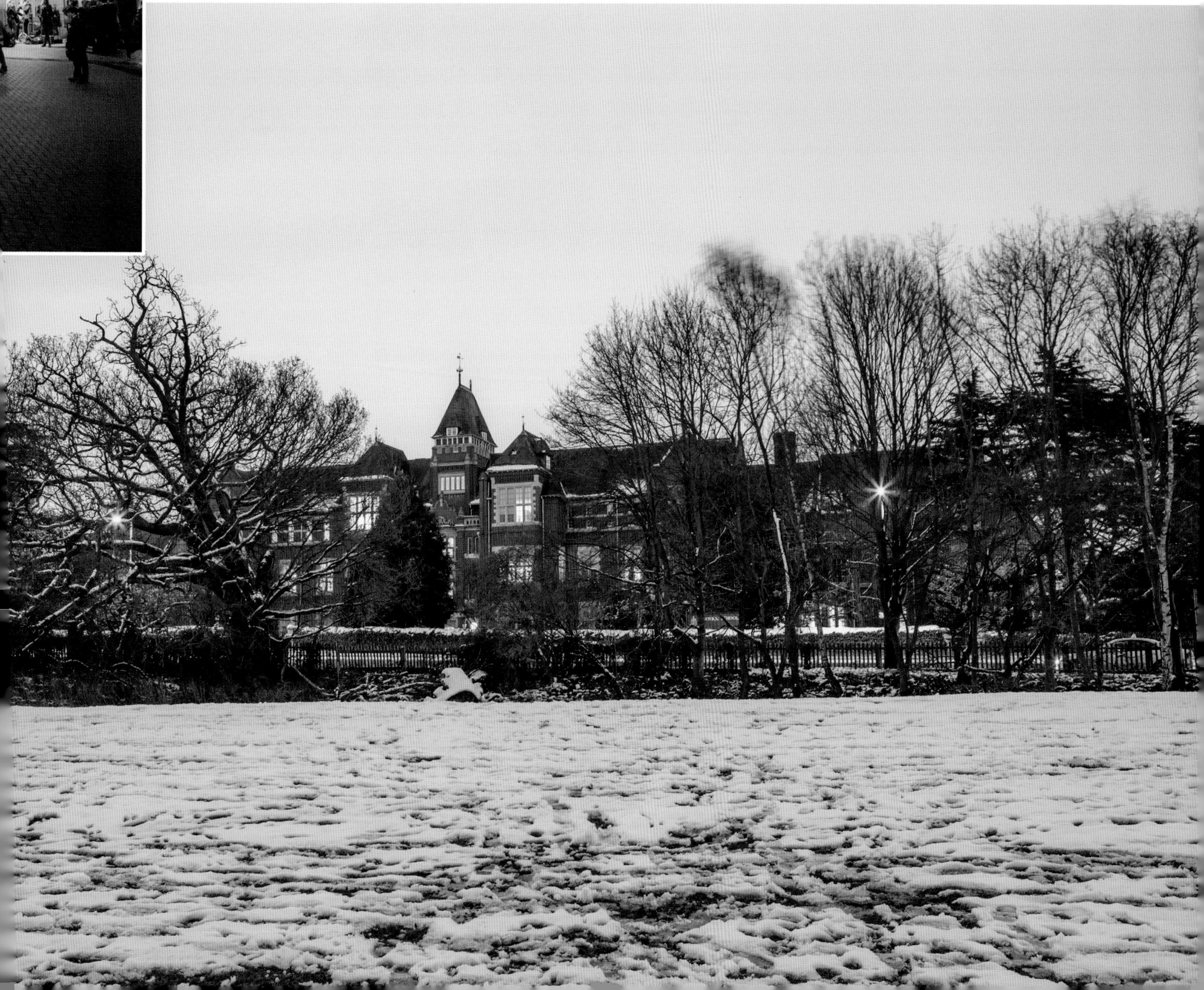

Peter Johnston, started Warwick School 16 September 1948.

One of our first administrative details to be carried out was to hand over our ration books to Warwick School. Most food was still rationed and someone spent a lot of time cutting out coupons for meat, cheese, fats and sugar.

– Peter Johnston, WS 1948–55

My over-riding impression of that first day remains the feeling of being a very small fish in a large sea, populated by masters in black gowns, other staff in brown cow gowns and tall, serious-looking prefects. The whole scene was accompanied by enough rules and regulations to trip up the unwary (even equipped with a copy of the School Code) which were issued when we wrote out our form timetable on the first morning of a seven-year stay at Warwick (never to be forgotten even 60 years later).

– Nigel Harris, started Warwick School 16 September 1952

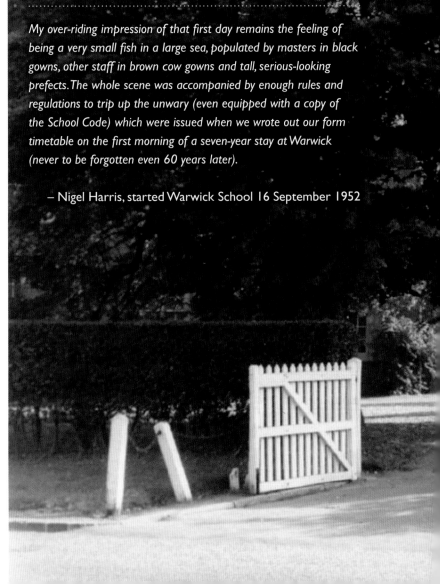

On the first day all new boys had to report to the bursar's stores to collect one cap badge, one blazer badge and three brass blazer buttons.

– **Peter Stocker**, started Warwick School 20 September 1946

Top: *Assembly with A.H.B. Bishop, 1961.*

Above: *A 1966 photograph staged to demonstrate the need for a new assembly hall.*

Above: *Assembly in Guy Nelson Hall, 1990s.*

Right: *Assembly, 2013.*

The Pirates of Penzance *at Warwick School in the late 1950s was produced by Mr R.P. Usherwood. I played Isabel, one of General Stanley's daughters, wearing a Kate Greenaway frock, a poke bonnet and my mother's beach shoes. I read in the Leamington Courier at that time that I, together with the other daughters (played by G.W. Price and C.J. Cruickshanks) made a tuneful trio. School productions such as* The Pirates of Penzance *enabled me, neither academic nor talented enough to be a school team sportsman, to express myself through the discipline, camaraderie and enjoyment of being part of an entertainments team. I have never worn a dress since, but still take every opportunity to sing.*

— Nicholas Whiting, WS 1956–63

Left: Treasure Island, *1930s.*

Below: Coram Boy, *2009.*

Above: Les Misérables, *2007.*

Above middle: Patience, *1974.*

Left: Pirates of Penzance, *1959.*

Right: Guys and Dolls, *2010.*

Above: 1961 school orchestra.

Left: Orchestra from Jesus Christ Superstar, 2012.

Peewit (Major Whitlam) lived at the school in the tower of the main building. There he held gramophone concerts of classical music on Saturday evenings for the senior boarders.

– **John Cooper**, WS 1940–49

Boarding House cubicles, 1923.

Boarding House bedrooms, 1990s.

As a ten-year-old boarder, my prized possessions were my Stuart Surridge cricket bat, autographed by England skipper, Peter May, and a small Pye radio. The radio came with an exceedingly uncomfortable earpiece – essential for listening after lights out. In senior boarding house, radio became increasingly important to us all.

*– **Nigel Kay**, WS 1957–68*

One bath per week. There was a painted line in the bath to ration the amount of water used.

*– **John Cooper**, WS 1940–49*

My favourite memories are of winter evenings in Junior Boarding House, sitting in our slippers and dressing gowns while Matron Ros Wilson (née Pulford) made us hot chocolate in front of her fire and read to us from 101 Dalmatians. Then off to bed and a goodnight kiss for each of us from that wonderful lady.

*– **Nigel Robinson**, WS 1955–66*

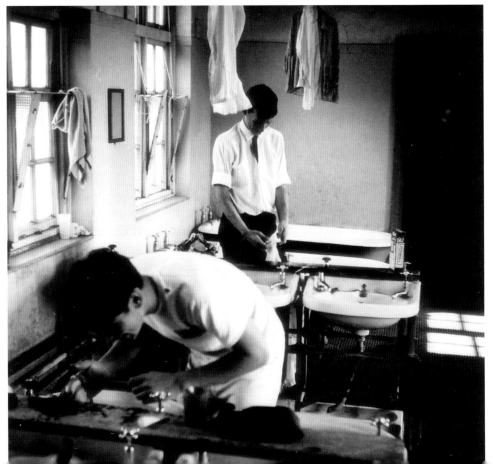

Boarding washroom, 1968.

Top: *A bird's-eye view — boarding room cubicles, 1985.*

Above: *Dormitory, 1966.*

Right: *Boarding House, 2013.*

Above: WS Rugby, 1934–35: believed to be the first 'live action' rugby photo at the school.

During the Dig for Victory campaign for the war, some parts of the playing fields had been planted. This was still the case in 1948 and our first PT classes were potato picking. We had to dress in rugger shirts, shorts and boots and spend 45 minutes, twice a week, picking potatoes.

– Peter Johnston,
WS 1948–55

Every time I went to the Tuck Shop I was attracted to a 'naive' oil painting on the wall of a Warwick School 1st XV player running with the ball. I loved this picture and always aspired to emulate the anonymous player.
  – Mike Barnwell, WS 1st XV 1966, 1967 and captain 1968

Left: Daily Mail Cup U15 champions, Twickenham 2013.

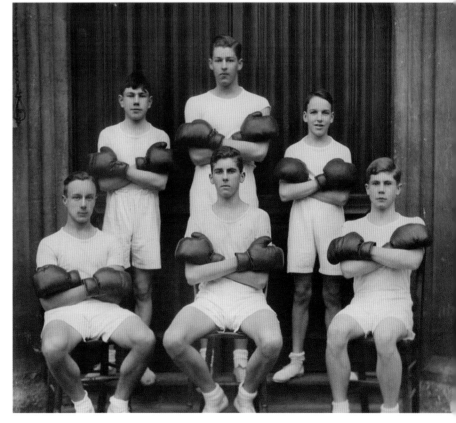

Top: *School vs OWs, umpired by John Strover, 1977.*

Above: *New Gym, 1960s.*

Above right: *Cross-country running, 1955.*

Right: *Boxing team, 1930s.*

The Town Crier's visit goes back until at least 1912.

Left: Early 1950s.

Below: 2007.

IN HONOUR OF OLD WARWICKIANS IN THE
ARMED FORCES WHO LOST THEIR LIVES
IN THE SERVICE OF THEIR COUNTRY
1945 ~

D. W. WHITE, died 1946, CEYLON
R. F. MUSGRAVE, died 1951, KOREA
J. J. WHITTAKER, died 2008, AFGHANISTAN

WE WILL REMEMBER THEM.

When you look at this memorial, remember first of all, in Joe's case, this is not history, this is now, and now in its rawest form. These were inspiring men of substance and they will have left a huge gap and that odd mixture of pride and sadness with their families.
— Maj. Gen. Mike Huntley CB, WS 1962–69

Top left: *1955 Church Parade.*

Left: *Remembrance Parade in Warwick, 2011.*

WARWICK SCHOOL.

THE GOVERNORS AND HEADMASTER

REQUEST THE PLEASURE OF YOUR COMPANY

AT WARWICK SCHOOL

FOR THE VISIT OF

**HER MAJESTY QUEEN ELIZABETH,
THE QUEEN MOTHER,**

ON THE MORNING OF

THURSDAY, 6TH NOVEMBER, 1958.

If you are able to come please reply to the Headmaster's Secretary by October 30th, stating the number of seats required in Big School, when tickets will be sent.

[P.T.O.

My father, H.C.G. Sawyer, taught maths and was Captain in the CCF. He lined up with the cadet corps on the day of the Queen Mother's visit. One of the Queen Mother's equerries had given strict instructions on royal etiquette. My father had been told to salute and then put his arm down. When the Queen Mother actually stopped to speak to him, he was so taken up with the moment that he spent the whole time talking to her while still saluting. It was only after she had moved on, with him still saluting, that someone pointed out he should take his hand down.

— Andrew Sawyer, WS 1952–64

The Queen Mother inspects the CCF during her visit in 1958.

I will never forget the Tuck Shop with its brick floor, oak tables with yellow-tiled tops and sepia photos of pre-war gym teams of Brooke and Leycester houses.

— **Nigel Harris**, WS 1952–59

A trip to the Tuck Shop would come with a lesson in manners – if not grammar. A request of 'Please can I have a cream bun?' would be met with 'Of course you can, but don't you want to ask if you may?' Infuriating to an eight year old, but effective.

— **Adrian Keeling QC**, WS 1975–85

Queuing for tuck, 1960s.

Food was not good. To this day I don't enjoy rice pudding or minced meat. There was also a tapioca pudding known publicly as frog spawn. The most peculiar dish was what was promoted as scrambled egg. This exactly resembled foam carpet underlay but was brown. It was, in fact, edible.

— **Anon**, WS 1950s

Tuck Shop, 1960s.

I seem to remember that in the early years at school, after the war, we had whale meat and 'snook' (fish) for lunch, but these things were matter of fact after the restrictions of the war years.
— **Joe Dunstan**, WS 1946–54

School House Supper, the annual event at the end of the Michaelmas term, was a great change from the ever-present cheese pie or egg and chips. There was no alcohol although the more senior boys would smuggle in gin and scotch to liven up the evening.
— **Anon**, early 1950s

Behind the scenes and on stage, Jesus Christ Superstar, *November 2012.*

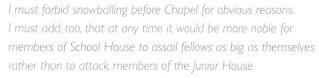

I must forbid snowballing before Chapel for obvious reasons.
I must add, too, that at any time it would be more noble for
members of School House to assail fellows as big as themselves
rather than to attack members of the Junior House.

— Revd J.P.Way, 1 Feb, 1895

Bonfire night gave great opportunities for fun. Around 1960, with over 100 boarders, there were lots of people sleeping in the main building, so riding pedal bicycles around the island in front of the main entrance at midnight, while holding fireworks, caused a few lights to come on.
– Norman Hyde, WS 1956–63

Above: *Chapel Choir, 1903.*　　　**Right:** *Carol Service, 2012.*

Below: Walking up to Carol Service, December 2012.   *Above:* Christmas in the Boarding House, 1970s.

Christmas Concert in the Guy Nelson Hall, 2012.

LENT

LENT

At the start of the Lent Term several Sixth Formers hear from Oxford and Cambridge Universities that they have an offer of a place. Each year the successful applicants duly line up for a photo taken by Peter O'Grady. The Master's Book of 1884 proudly recorded the scholarships of three boys at Oxford University, and each was used as an excuse to award the whole school a half day's

Top: *Oxbridge entrants, 2010.*   **Above:** *Oxbridge entrants, 1995.*

holiday. The vast majority of the Upper Sixth obtains offers from prestigious universities by the end of the year.

Entrance into Warwick School has always been selective one way or another. In 1571 it was stated that the school was only for boys who knew the elements of grammar. At that time an important distinction was made between boys born in Warwick and those from outside the borough. Only the former were taught free of charge.

The vast and varied curriculum today has developed over the years. Indeed, in the early 19th century pupils were said to have learnt nothing but Greek and Latin. In 1842, a new scheme for the regulation of the school stated clearly that 'the Usher or Undermaster should be appointed by the Headmaster', who should be 'competent to teach as well the Classics, Mathematics and the higher branches of arithmetic and should be well versed in Literature, Geography and Science'.

Along with a development of the subjects, the facilities and accommodation have improved dramatically over the years and have come a long way since 1832, when the school consisted of two large rooms.

Science is one area where these developments are most evident. The location of the original Chemistry laboratory was almost certainly the teaching room next to the Chapel. Governors' minutes from 1878 noted that the Headmaster was to be authorised to charge the pupils in the chemistry classes the cost of materials used in class experiments.

The first science block was built in 1905 at a cost of just over £1,000, and today that building houses the Music department. A new Science block was built in 1957 that housed the three departments until 2006. The building of a £6.1 million state-of-the-art Science Centre, named after Dr Cheshire, was completed in 2007.

Design and Technology is still housed in the original Engineering Shop, built in 1910, although the interior has been transformed over the years. Soon after its completion it was used to help produce munitions in the First World War, namely shell-cases and shell-caps.

March 2013 saw the opening of the Halse Sports Pavilion, the latest in the line of facility upgrades. This was officially opened by

Lord Coe and was a fitting tribute to Edward Halse in his final year at Warwick School. The first gymnasium in the school, now the Sixth Form Centre, was opened in 1890 and the outdoor swimming pool, opened in 1911, was replaced by a modern indoor pool and sports centre in 1992.

School lunches have long been a focal point of school life. The dining room started in one of the three rooms used today and 15 of the oak tables made in the school workshop in 1901 are still in use. There are many carved inscriptions in the Panel Room (the original 1879 dining room) and these panels were available to purchase at 10/6 per panel plus 2d per letter but were particularly aimed at pupils 'whose names being absent from scholarship panels and sporting photographs… would otherwise fade from history'.

Fetching water at Camp, Abbots Salford, 1940.

Many of the boarders still remember in detail the food they ate. During the Second World War rations were limited and a particular issue was egg allocation, which was limited to one boiled egg per month! Today food is far more varied and plentiful, with a choice of three menus daily. Boarders now have the opportunity to prepare their own snacks in kitchenettes.

In modern times, there has always been a Tuck Shop and in 1932 a replacement was created in the 'old bicycle house'. It was, as today, a popular destination at break. In 1938 buns were sold at a cost of one penny each and rock cakes and custards at 1½d, each which resulted in a stampede at the Tuck Shop.

Today, the Lent term is extremely busy for the musicians, with concerts performed weekly. Jazz at the Bridge has become a large event featuring all the school's jazz musicians. This contrasts greatly with the early 1960s, when the Head of Music disapproved of the excessive growth, as he saw it, of interest in woodwind and brass and supported the cause of the strings!

The rugby season continues into the Lent term, often ending with a run in the Daily Mail Cup. The trophy proved elusive until 2007 when the 1st XV won the title, followed by the U15 XV in 2013, both played at Twickenham, in front of a large crowd of school supporters. The Sevens season, including the long-standing Warwick School Sevens tournament, runs at the end of Lent term.

The Annual CCF review takes place at the end of term, when the Combined Cadet Force is inspected by a high-ranking officer. The CCF has a long and valued history at Warwick. Old

Chapel Quad, 1961.

Warwickian Colonel Samuel William Cooke deserves to be remembered as the founder of the school's Cadet Corps in 1884. The Cadet Corps later became attached to the Second Battalion of the Royal Warwickshire Regiment, and by the late 1880s probably every boy in the school joined when he reached

the age of 12. The OTC (Officer's Training Corps) was actually on camp the day the First World War broke out, but had to end early as 'mobilisation deprived us of most of the cooks'. By 1915 all of the OTC's rifle and bayonets had been called in by the War Office.

The Junior Training Corps and Air Training Corps (from 1941) had more than justified their existence in the years up to 1945. In 1945 the JTC took part in the Victory Parade in Warwick and was inspected by Field Marshal Montgomery in 1947. A pre-CCF was created for younger candidates in 1964 and an RAF contingent was introduced which soon had 50 cadets, not far short of the Army section. Camps and Arduous Training took place across the UK and an indoor rifle range was opened on the school site.

In 2003 four KHS girls joined the CCF. The CCF has continued to offer a wide variety of outside activities at many locations, with Adventurous Training in the Lake District being an annual favourite.

Whilst extra-curricular activities have long formed part of life at Warwick School, it was in the early 20th century that the programme was expanded, with the formation of Cycling and Chess Clubs and a School Fire Brigade, whilst developing further the Natural History Society, the Photographic Society and the Shakespeare Society. Debating is one of the more established societies, with the earliest reference to debating at Warwick School in the late 19th century.

Above: *Junior School, 1979.*

Warwick School holds happy memories for me. I enjoyed my time there, learnt a great deal and formed life-long friendships.
— Christian Horner OBE, WS 1987–92

*Boys relaxing between lessons, 2013 (**above**) and 1912 (**right**).*

A Sunday afternoon would be appointed for a race to Stratford or three times round the Tachbrook triangle. The Saturday afternoon before would be engaged in dismantling, lubricating and tuning up our assorted bikes.

— Anon, WS in the 1960s

Above: *Boarders' bike race, 1958.*

Left: *Pool, 1974.*

Far left: *Table tennis, 1968.*

Recreation facilities, for the boarders, consisted of two common rooms, one for seniors (14–18) and the other for juniors (11–13). There was a daily paper in the junior common room. The only wireless available was in the senior common room. Programmes were monitored by the house prefects. A table tennis table and French billiard table were situated in the games room and were much in demand.

— John Cooper, WS 1940–49

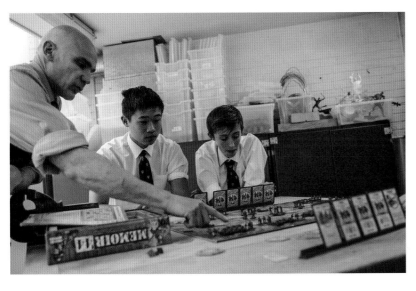

Right: Masters' Common Room, 1969.

Left: H.S. Pyne and masters, c.1906.

Left: Staff marking Sixth Form projects, 2013

Above: Staff on Charity Walk, 2002.   *Right:* Staff Common Room, 2013.

Jazz at the Bridge, February 2013.

Warwick School was and still is a magnificent institution full of inspirational teachers. Pupils were given the opportunity to reach their full potential academically and encouraged to develop other skills in areas such as sport and music. I was given opportunities to try many things and found my passion in the debating society, which gave me a grounding for my future career. I have fond memories of being a chorister and singing in chapel as part of the school choir. I look upon the school with a wonderful warm heart and think how lucky I was to be part of such an inspiring community.

— Harry Greenway, WS 1946–53. Conservative MP for Ealing North 1979–97

He was subject unto them

I ascend My Father unto and your Father

IN MEMORIAM CECILI MEGGS D·D·PARENTES

1545

Altiora

ALTIORA PETO.

WARWICK 1 2
VISITORS 0 0

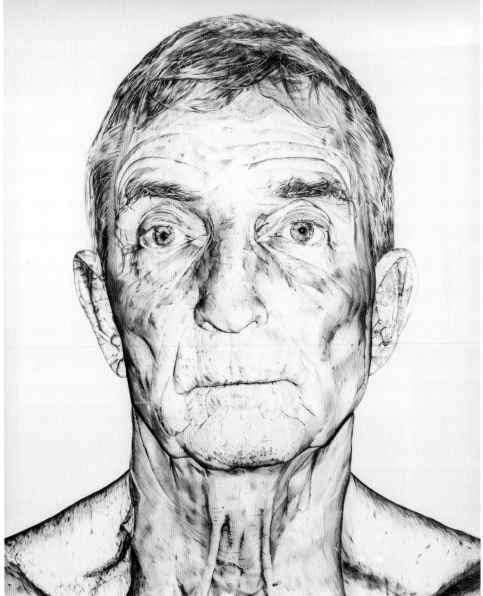

Collection of
modern artwork.

Trousers had to be a uniform grey. I remember coming back after a holiday with a lovely baggy light grey pair and was promptly told to go and change them.

— **Revd Bill Allander**, WS 1926–32

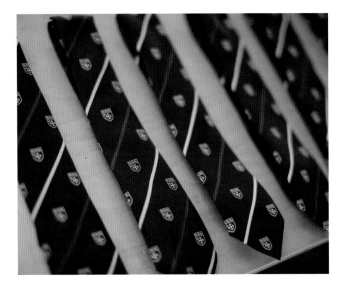

Above: Junior School prefects' ties.

Above: Sixth Formers, 2013.

In 1948 the uniform consisted of grey flannel shorts and shirts, long grey stockings and a navy blue raincoat. We were also allowed a navy suit for Sunday. By the Lower Fifth practically everyone wore long trousers. With the move into long trousers came a change in shirts — these were now white with separate collars. We were allowed one shirt and two collars per week. As a boarder, underwear and socks were changed on Wednesdays. Pyjamas had to last a fortnight. School uniform was also frequently worn in the holidays, as clothing may still have been rationed. During the summer term, those who were in the Upper Fifth or Sixth forms were allowed to wear a boater in place of the school cap.

— **Peter Johnston**, WS 1948–55

In those days, we still wore caps, mainly so that the older boys could steal them and throw them at each other. The hard brims meant they worked like proto-Frisbees. We all carried leather satchels, so full of exercise books and textbooks that we had to move, crab-like, in a sideways direction as none of us had the strength to move in a straight line. I still have one shoulder that is higher than the other.

— **John Cavanagh QC**, WS 1968–78

Summer uniform, 1945.

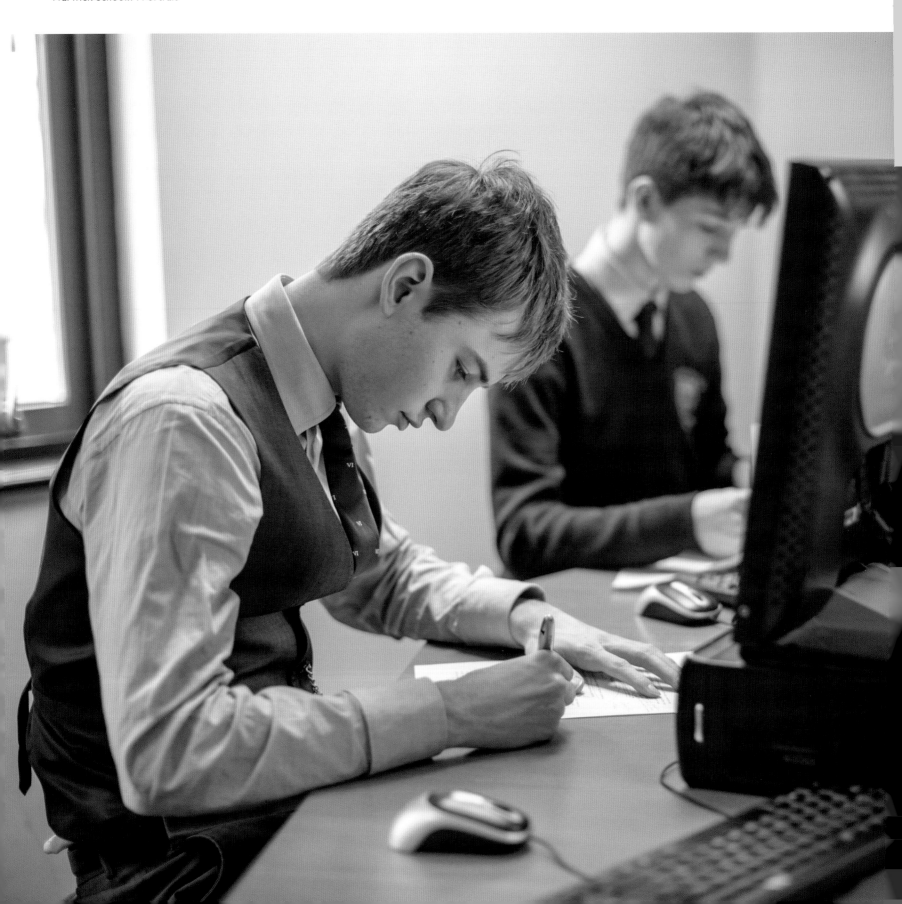

Today there are computers everywhere, instead of the single school computer which was the pride and joy of the Maths Department. Boys no longer carry slide rules in grey boxes. Boys no longer have to crack the ice in order to swim in the outside pool on a cold April day.

— **John Cavanagh QC**, WS 1968–78

Above: Junior School, 1979.

Below: The first computer room, 1986.

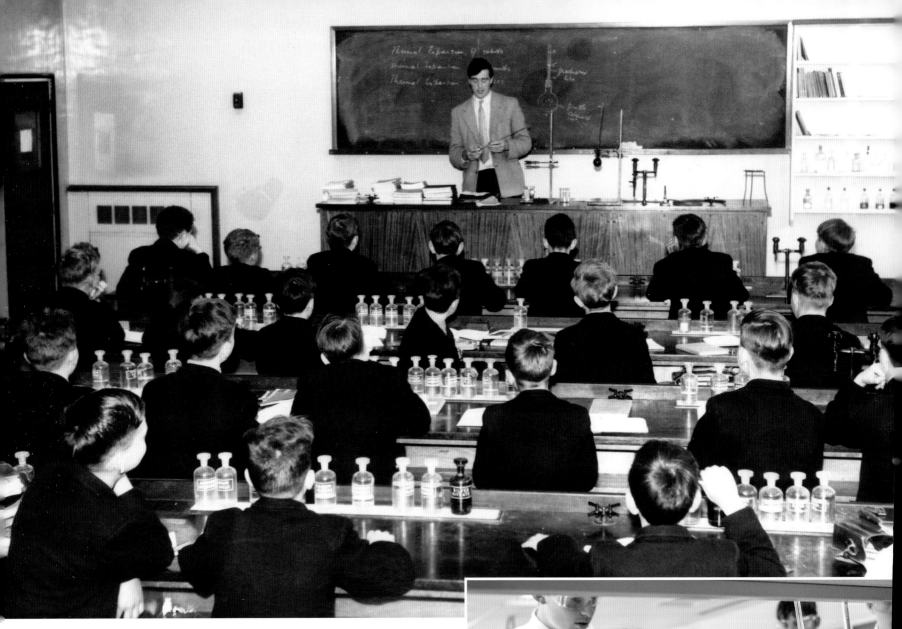

Chemistry, 1963.

The Revd Hector Cullis was famous for his coal mine experiment, intended to demonstrate the effect of the ignition of 'firedamp' in coal mines. The apparatus consisted of a long narrow box with a hinged door at each end. It was equipped with a gas pipe and a sparking plug. The plug was fired using a coil and battery. The gas was let in and the plug fired, with the 'experimental' result being the inevitable explosion with an impressive tongue of flame erupting from each end of the box. The tale goes that on one occasion, most unwisely, H.C. stood at the end instead of the side and set fire to himself.

— Anon

Design and technology is still housed in the engineering shop, built in 1910.

The library was a mine of information. The favourite book was the 1914 edition of Jane's Fighting Ships. This initiated some fantastic designs for fighting vessels and probably gave us the idea for the games of battleships we played on squared paper at the end of term.

-- **Anon**, WS in the 1950s

'Cas' Warren, Geography master, liked to lean on a tall, narrow, roll-front cabinet. He was not so happy when we placed marbles underneath it. His wall-mounted, pull-down map of the world caused fun when we had earlier unwound it and filled it with confetti-like pieces of paper. He looked like a bride-groom when next he opened it.

-- **Norman Hyde**, WS 1956–63

Looking at the ceiling for no reason, when being taught, was always popular. This was set up by just one boy looking up, then nudging his neighbour and so on until so many were actively involved that the master had to cast a glance upwards.

— **Norman Hyde**, WS 1956–63

Left: Joe Dunstan, WS 1947–54, going off to CCF camp.

My father was so proud of this picture that he had it framed and displayed on the wall of his office when he was Administrator of the Royal Midland Counties Home in Leamington.

My friend John Buckley and I had only recently joined the JTC and, like all recruits, had been equipped with old WWI uniforms, which included Forage Caps and puttees like the ones used in the trenches. The whole Corps was in the process of converting to the modern uniforms and we two were the only stand-outs. The day before Monty's visit it was decided that we should be 'converted' too. My mother did her best but there was no way to shrink mine down in time. Hence the baggy appearance. We had been forewarned that Monty was likely to speak to either the tallest or the shortest member. As I was by far the smallest, he picked on me. I was too overawed to remember what he said or what I replied.

— Douglas Badger, WS 1944–51

Field Marshal Montgomery on his 1947 visit to the school. Douglas Badger is pictured talking to Monty, second from right.

Above: Mid 1950s general inspection parade.

During parade, 'Monty' poked me on the chest with his finger and with considerable force stated in no uncertain terms that my shirt was a cricket shirt as opposed to an army issue one.

— John Taylor, WS 1952–58

Right: Colonel Bob Carruthers OBE TD, inspects the CCF, March 2013.

SUMMER

SUMMER

Summer is a term of contrasts, with the intensity of exams followed by relative freedom for many at the end of term. In the first half the more senior boys face their external exams, and the younger ones sit internal exams.

Early in the Summer term, therefore, the Upper Sixth prepare to leave the school for exam leave. Leavers' Day is a relatively recent phenomenon which starts with breakfast and distribution of the Yearbooks and includes a chapel service and inter-form tug of war. More traditionally boys, for many years, went to the Banbury Road bridge and threw their caps into the river. It was said that, to keep the Earl of Warwick happy, the School Bursar had to go to the river with a long pole and fish out as many caps as he could!

Academic performance and results have always been a measure of performance at Warwick School and a focus for each Headmaster. Revd William Grundy, who became Headmaster in 1881, employed a technique with idle boys, which was to put the bottom two boys in each class on a 'satisfecit', and if they had not improved in a fortnight, they were flogged. These lists, or Form Orders, were read out in Big School on Saturdays and the floggings took place shortly afterwards in the Headmaster's study. The term Form Order is still used, and those lower down the lists are put 'on report', but no longer flogged!

U14 XI, 1900, the first ever U14 team.

Above left: F.A.L. Johnson arriving at school, 1904.

Left: Sports Day, 1990s.

Warwick School's chief examiner reported the following after the brief tenure of Revd Philip Edwin Raynor in 1885: 'I regret very much that there seems to be such a falling off this year in the general results. I trust that the new Headmaster will soon be able to stimulate Forms V and IV to more industry. I trust also that he will be able to improve the relaxed discipline so that the work of the viva-voce may be more easy and more pleasant.'

It seems this situation did indeed improve, and by 1906 two Warwick School boys were first in all England in Scripture and Greek in the Oxford Local exams.

Summer sports are dominated by cricket, tennis and athletics. The annual Sports Day has taken place since its introduction in the late 19th century.

Cricket at the school dates back to at least 1848, and along with rugby constituted 'small games'. In 1887 the Headmaster organised an army of pupils to level the cricket pitch which up to that point appeared to have had medieval-type ridges. Despite falling numbers at the school in 1900, Warwick School fielded three cricket teams, the 1st XI, 2nd XI and the U14 XI, but staff often played in the senior teams to make up the numbers. The Second World War had inevitable far-reaching effects on the provision of equipment, and this impacted upon the sports department. Cricket was limited to seven balls for the whole season and getting playable pitches relied upon the good nature of the remaining ground staff.

Sports Day, early 1930s.

Swimming was a popular activity during the summer term. The bathing place used by the school until 1911 is marked on old maps – a segment of the River Avon was diverted through a pool on the far side of the river, almost opposite the school. In 1911 the school opened its long-awaited outdoor swimming pool. This was used right up until it was filled in in 1991. Swimming now takes place at the inside pool. Warwick School boys undertook the challenge of the Channel Swim Relay in 2006 and have now completed this crossing three times, including the two-way crossing in 2012, the only school to have completed such a challenge to date.

The Duke of Edinburgh Award scheme has been popular for decades and, more recently, record numbers have enrolled for the 'Gold Award'.

Whilst sport at the school has developed over the years, one sport disappeared for many. A boxing class was first offered in 1905 and for years the OTC cadets took part in competitions whilst on camp but it was 1930 before the sport featured officially at Warwick School, and lasted until the Second World War.

Trips and tours now take place all year round. The first school trip abroad took place in 1929 when an expedition was undertaken to Dunkirk, Brussels, Bruges and Ghent. However it appears trips did not run smoothly in those days. There was a collision between a German tanker and the ship on which the Warwick School boys travelled, and on the same trip a student was allegedly offered a 'bière' instead of a 'billet' in a café. Trips were temporarily abandoned. Fortunately, they are now an established part of school life, with trips and tours taking place across the world every year.

Speech Day, 1968.

The Summer term ends with Prizegiving and Speeches for both the Junior and Senior Schools. Frequently the prizes are awarded by an eminent visitor, who may be an OW. Over the many years the list of guests has been long and impressive. The messages imparted to the boys have been varied too, including an interesting approach from the Poet Laureate, John Masefield OW, who in 1928 told a packed Chapel 'I hope all you boys are happy here. I wasn't – I ran away'.

This formal event has for many years followed a similar format, with staff and governors seated on stage in front of the prize-winning students and their parents. Staff line up at the back of the Guy Nelson Hall and walk onto the stage to be seated. In 1906, the teachers of Music, Art and Woodwork were considered non-academic staff and not rated as important enough to be on stage for Speech Day!

In 1935 an experimental outdoor Speech Day was ruined by a violent and drenching thunderstorm.

For the governors of the school, Speech Day is one of many events they attend. The board of governors was created in 1842 consisting of the Earl of Warwick, the Recorder of Warwick, the Mayor of Warwick, two representatives of the Town Council and two representatives of the trustees who should be visitors of the school.

The formal presentations are followed by refreshments with governors, staff and parents entertained in the Headmaster's garden – a hospitable end to the school year.

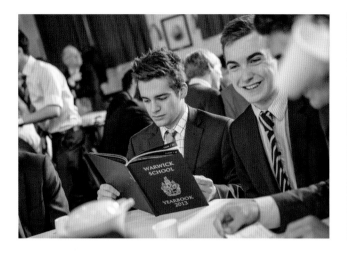

Below: Pupils throwing their caps in the river on the last day of school, 1963.

Sixth Form Leavers' Day, May 2013.

When the time came to leave Warwick I could hardly bear to go. I had a deep affection for the place.
– D.E.R. Scarr, WS 1931–38

My most abiding memory from my time at Warwick was lining up along the main corridor before morning chapel, in descending form order, sixth formers outside the then history classroom — now where the school office is, down to the Lower Fourths along the side corridor, supervised by Geoffrey Simmonds. At the appointed time the Headmaster — A.H.B. Bishop — would emerge from his study, gown flowing and carrying his mortarboard, walking down the corridor into chapel, but carefully noting untidy hair or dirty shoes on his way! As soon as the boys were nearly all in chapel the staff would come down their staircase and follow into chapel.

— Peter Bailey, WS 1942–49

*My fondest memory is playing cricket in the nets,
straight after prep in Junior Boarding House.*
— Julian Ball, WS 1978–86

*My most abiding annual happy memory of Warwick School was the smell of cut grass
at the start of the summer term: it heralded the beginning of the cricket season. I was
Captain of the 1st XI in 1967. I took a few wickets but sadly did not really prosper with
the bat, though I did get 61 not out in my first innings as Captain which included two
sixes over the wicket-keeper's head into The Limes.*

— **The Hon. Sir David Foskett**, WS 1956–67,
Old Warwickian Association President 2000 and 2014

Top left: Net practice, 1963

Left: Old Warwickians 1st XI, 1910.

Left: 1980s javelin.   *Above: 1900 playing field.*   *Below: 1940s Sports Day.*

During the summer of 1940, because of conscription, there was a shortage of farm labourers. Groups of schoolboys were sent daily to help on the farms. During the summer holidays there were harvesting camps and instructional classes for tractor-driving and thatching.

As 90 per cent of boys couldn't go away for their holidays, the school was kept open. The programme was to be Roll Call and Chapel at 9am, and then farming or games (cricket, tennis, fives and swimming). The shooting ranges were in constant use, while the boys over 17 formed their own platoon of Home Guards and patrolled every night. Boys were to come in 'holiday garb' too – a real innovation as one could ordinarily be punished for failing to wear the school cap. The school was somewhat dumbfounded, but Mr Bishop stressed his point by announcing that, 'if you observe me conducting chapel in my mortar board and my bathing slips (startled gasps), you will know that I am in a holiday mood' (cheers).

– Don Chutter, WS 1940

Boys on the playing field with the Cheshire Science Centre and its photovoltaic panels in the background.

Cleaning the pool in the 1960s.

My other memory of A.H.B. Bishop is a distant view of him in a magnificent Victorian swimming costume, black and white striped, covering him from neck to knee. The staff would be allowed to use the swimming pool in the early evening.

— Anon

During the summer term we were able to use the swimming pool, under supervision. This is where I learnt to swim. The pool had no filtration system. The senior boarders would, at the start of the summer term, empty the pool and scrub down the floor and walls.

— **John Cooper**, WS 1940–49

1947.

1920.

During the summer term 'Chips' (the legendary Mr Usherwood) would go for a daily morning swim and everyone was welcome. He used to go round each dorm before the morning wake up bell, gently open the door and whisper 'swim'. Those who wished, would rush downstairs, get changed and tiptoe gingerly across the gritty junior playground. Once at the pool, Chips would already be ploughing back and forth down the centre. It was even better if it was raining!

— Andrew Mead, WS 1979–86

Sports Day, July 2013.

Left: *1980s egg and spoon race.*

Right: *Rugby international Tim Dalton in the relay, 1950s.*

Above: Olympic gold medal winner A.G.K. Brown in the long jump, 1933.

Left: Snowdonia, 1966.

Below: World Challenge – Kyrgyzstan, 2009.

Above: World Challenge – Bolivia, 2007.

Left: Adventurous Training, 2009.

Left: Field trip to Arran, 1960s.

Below: 100-mile charity walk, 2009.

When I first heard about the 100-mile charity walk, I have to admit I was somewhat apprehensive but before I knew it I was on the school minibus bound for Wales on Easter Monday! After six days of hills, sheep and blisters and some excellent banter we made it from Abergavenny to Aberystwyth. The support I received made the challenge both worthwhile and rewarding – from the awesome hill climb on the first day to dipping my sore feet in the Irish Sea on the last!

– Gerard Rhodes, WS 2002–13

Teaching staff, 2002.

Teaching staff, 1977.

Left: Ralph Thornton's retirement, 1989.

Below: Longest-serving members of Warwick School, 2013.

Examinations, June 2013.

If shooting had been going well on the lunchtime team practices you would hear this sort of exchange: 'Sir, sir, there's a fly on my target, can I shoot it?' P. Whitlam: 'Dammit, only if you hit it.'
— **Revd Andrew Stevens**, WS 1955–63

On some Saturday afternoons Peewit (Major Whitlam) would organise team practice at Wedgnock Range. We were issued .303 Enfield rifles at the school armoury and would then cycle through Warwick to the firing range, with the rifles strapped to our backs.
— **John Cooper**, WS 1940–49

I thoroughly enjoyed my days with the JTC. When we went out on exercises we would be issued with denims. One day I was given the Bren gun to carry. I put its heavy magazine in the front pocket of my trousers but as the denims were too large for me my trousers kept falling down as we marched along.
— **Ronnie Raymond-Cox**, WS 1944–46

MOD & NON MOD PERSONNEL
WHEN RED LIGHT IS ON...
FIRING IS IN PROGRESS
DO NOT ENTER

pp130–1: *Staff assembling before Speech Day, July 2013.*

Speech Day, July 2013.

HEAD OF THE SCHOOL

OLD WARWICKIANS

1969-70 M.J.JORDAN	1985-6 C.J.FREEMAN
1970-1 B.D.JOSEPH	86-7 M.J.JORDAN
1971-2 W.H.WILSON	1987-8 A.C.W.LAPSLEY
1972-3 R.B.SEATON	1988-9 A.N.H.HUGHES
1973-4 M.A.HINTON	1989-90 J.H.NEALE
1974-5 B.J.WHITLOCK	1990-1 S.R.HUCKER
1975-6 R.J.C.LAING	1991-2 B.W.HUDSON
1976-7 J.A.M.JORDAN	1992-3 A.N.JORDAN
1977-8 P.T.GREENHILL	1993-4 A.WEST
1978-9 C.A.LAMMIE	1994-5 S.D.WURR
1979-80 J.W.HASSAN	1995-6 P.S.CHAPLIN
1980-1 M.G.SHORTHOSE	1996-7 T.I.WURR
1981-2 A.J.LORD	1997-8 T.J.J.McKAY
1982-3 J.P.FREEMAN	1998-9 S.J.FRAMPTON
1983-4 T.C.WHITEHEAD	1999-00 M.E.BUCKWORTH
1984-5 S.A.LOVEGROVE	2000-01 G.PACITTI
	2001-02 J.J.T.SHINKWIN
	2002-03 O.G.JAMES

HEAD OF SCHOOL HOUSE

1969-70	P.L.WEISSBERG
1970-1	B.D.JOSEPH
1971-2	R.C.BARNWELL
1972-3	J.E.DUTTON
1973-4	G.A.HAWKESFORD
1974-5	I.R.HENSON
1975-6	L.HINDE
1976-7	C.J.DENT
1977-8	K.D.LESLIE
1978-9	W.N.ALDRIDGE
1979-80	C.H.FLOWER
1980-1	I.CHALEB
1981-2	J.St.G.SHACKLOCK
1982-3	T.M.COLE
1983-4	R.A.C.STEPHENS
1984-5	S.A.LOVEGROVE
1985-6	M.J.BLAKE
1986-7	J.N.BEACHUS
1987-8	R.N.BEATTIE
1988-9	P.M.A.HULYER
1989-90	I.R.CRUICKSHANKS
1990-1	B.D.GUEST
1991-2	D.A.BYLES
1992-3	S.P.SHINER
1993-4	R.J.RUPARELLIA
1994-5	J.E.DORR
1995-6	C.J.COLLET
1996-7	R.M.THORPE
1997-8	M.B.COLLET
1998-9	R.DICKIE
1999-00	A.BUCK
2000-01	J.P.BEGG
2001-02	J.J.T.SHINKWIN
2002-03	M.AHER

Above: 1969 Leavers' Reunion, 2009.

Below: The Old Warwickian Association 1st XV, December 1960, for the annual match against the school.

Above: OWA Past Presidents' Dinner, 2011   *Below:* The annual London Reunion.

Friendships maintained and rediscovered at Old Warwickian events and reunions are truly special.

— **Roy Dixon**, WS 1973–81, OWA Chairman 2011–14

Happy memories? Three parts in three school plays: Verges in Much Ado About Nothing, *Water Rat in* Toad of Toad Hall *and 'Stumper' Selincourt in* Penny for a Song. *Sad memories? The untimely deaths of Angus Wainwright and Roger Banham (who was Mole in* Toad of Toad Hall*) in road traffic accidents on Myton Road. They have never had the opportunity of fulfilling their potential in life and of sharing the reunions in which the rest of us share. Other better memories? Some inspirational staff – Ralph Thornton, 'Tom' Long and 'Chips' Usherwood to name but a few – who must have passed on something that has led to some modest success in my career. To the whole institution, thank you, and long may it flourish.*

— **The Hon. Sir David Foskett**, WS 1956–67, Old Warwickian Association President, 2000 and 2014

One of the moments of the Diamond Jubilee Lunch in 2012 was to meet up with my form mistress in 2B from 1947, Margaret Keighley, née Tingle.
— **David Millard**, WS 1946–55

Above: *OWA President's Dinner, Tower of London, 2013.*

Below: *1940s and 1950s Reunion, 2009.*

LIST OF SUBSCRIBERS

Harry Abell	2003–14	George Bates	2006–13
Chris Allen	1952–58	Oliver Bates	1984–95
Matthew Allen	2011–	C. Baumfield	
B.E. Allman	1992–99	John Bausor	1951–57
Thomas Richard Jonathan Ambler	2004–	J.C. (Toby) Beaufoy	1963–74
Reuben S.K. Arnold	2011–	Oliver Becque-Smith	2007–
Ian Ascroft	1996–01	Ronald Beech	1955–63
Enzo Anthony Ashe	2013–	Will Beech	2009–
Killian Josef Ashe	2012–	Michael Beeston	1943–48
Aaron K.J. Ashley	2002–09	Patrick Beevers	2011–
Aubrey A.R. Ashley	2008–	William E.W. Bell	2013–
Harlan A.R. Ashley	2000–07	Cliff Bellerby	1949–58
Richard Ashley	1943–50	Charlie Bend	1969–76
Haydn Ashworth	2010–	Charlie Benson	2008–
Louis Ashworth	2002–13	Jack Bentley	2010–
Toby Ashworth	2004–	Eur. Ing. Paul D. Bethel	1958–65
Tom Ashworth	2000–11	Kieran Bhogal	2010–
Jonathan Atack	1975–82	Thomas Bickerton	2008–13
Mark Avery	1992–96	J. Geoffrey Binks	1942–48
Douglas V. Badger	1944–51	Henry Birks	2004–
Leigh Baildham	1968–79	James Blake	1975–86
Joe Bain	2012–	Joe Blake	2003–14
Daniel Henry Bainbridge	2010–	Keir Blake	2000–11
Peter Baird	1953–61	Simon Blake	1999–11
Ian Baker	1954–63	Simon Blake	1973–84
Navrit J.S. Bal	2005–12	In memory of Tony Blakeman and	
Jonathan Ball	1971–82	Tim Spence 1942–52 and 1946–54	
Michael Ballard	2003–14	Professor Robert Bluglass CBE	1943–48
William Banfield	2009–	Joshua Bluteau	2002–09
J. and M. Banks	2008–	Sam Bluteau-Tait	2008–
Luke Barker	2013–	Clive Boast	1956–63
Matthew C. Barlow	2008–	Geoffrey Bodker	1934–40
Morgan J. Barnden	2008–	Christopher Bolton	2010–
Joseph Barnes	2010–	Peter Borsada	2008–
Samuel Barnes	2010–	Jack Bottomley	2005–12
Theodore J. Barnes	2013–	Stuart Botwright	1980–85
Michael Edward Barnwell	1960–68	Oliver Philip Bowden	1988–95
Riordan Barry	2009–	Douglas Boyle	2011–
Anton Bates	1953–60	Edward J. Brading	2011–

Alexander Bray	2009–	Nicholas C.E. Chesher	2006–13
Charles Bray	2009–	Aaron Hiu Chun Cheung	2012–
William Bray	2009–	Anthony Choy	2010–14
Katrina Briggs	2008–	Andrew Chung	2005–11
Matthew Bristow	1993–97	Justin Chung	2005–
Jack Bromwich	2008–	Arran David Clark	2012–
Ted Bromwich	2011–	Ian T. Clark	1971–78
Richard Brough	2008–	Tobias Clark	2010–
William Broughton	2012–	Roger Clarke	1981–88
Jill Brown		James Cleary	2004–
Robbie Brown	2012–	Harry Coley-Smith	2012–
Michael Buckland	2009–13	Jonathan Collett	1967–77
William Buckley	2011–	Colliver Family	2002–
David Bull	1980–86	Edward C. Commander	1984–91
George Burbidge	2005–13	Edward J. Commander	2011–
Benjamin Burrows	2011–	A.D.L. Cook	1972–79
Alex Burton	2012–	J.P. Cook	1982–89
Nigel R. Burton	1962–67	Jonathan Cook	1971–76
Jack Butler	1967–74	John Cooper	1940–49
Nicholas Butler	1985–92	Tom Cooper-Cocks	2002–09
Richard William Butler	1987–96	Roger Court	1951–58
Daniel Buxton	2011–	Peter Crafter	1967–71
Alexander Bywater	2001–08	Brian Croome	1949–55
Lawrence Bywater	2002–09	Adam David Cross	1995–05
M.J. Calderbank	1971–76	Joe Crossan	2005–10
Will Callan	2014–	William Alfred (Bill) Crouch	1940–46
Harvey Campbell	2001–	Alex Crummett	2010–
Jay Campbell	2001–	Liam Culbertson	2008–
Trevor J. Cardall	1947–53	James G.J. Cumberland	2001–10
Dominic Carrick	1981–92	James Paul Spencer Cunliffe	2011–13
Jack Carson	2012–	Dr Arnold E. Currall	1936–42
Henry Catchpole	2006–	Kieran Curran	2011–
John Cavanagh	1968–78	Tom Curtis	2005–
Dan Chambers	2012–	Christopher D'Este-Hoare	1993–98
Matt Chambers	2012–	Leo da Cruz	2012–
Edwin Chan	2012–	Cliff Daniel	WS Staff 1970–05
Joseph Chapman	2006–	Lt Col F.A.F. Daniell	Bursar 1986–01
Kevin Cheng	2009–14	Nicholas Dann	1971–82
Matthew C.E. Chesher	2000–07	Julian Darby	2006–13

Peter David	1947–51	Dr R.W. Fair	WS Staff 1977–04	Freddy Gretton	2009–
Owain Davies-McCrorie	2009–	Edward Farrimond	2011–13	Patrick D. Grinnell	1952–62
Anthony Oliver Davies	1968–75	Bailey Fear	2008–	Brian Groser	1940–44
Ralph Barry Davies	1956–65	Jacob Fenwick	2007–	Eric Hadley	
Jeremy Davis	1981–91	Ian Ferry	1978–83	WS Staff 1990–11 and 2013–14	
J.P.H. Davy	1941–46	Richard Ferry	1943–45	James Hadley	1982–92
S.R.P. Dawes	1978–87	Harrison Findlay-Smith	2012–	Brian Haimes	1945–54
James Scott-Dawkins	2012–	Robin Flintoff	WS Staff 1978–	Charles F.T. Hain	1999–10
Kristian Scott-Dawkins	2012–	James Foote	2010–	Christopher J.T. Hain	1973–80
Jack Gaudier Dean	2006–14	Neil Forsdyke	1970–80	Derrick Hain	1933–36
Edward DeArmitt	2006–	David Foskett	1956–67	Henry W.T. Hain	1915–18
Eric DeArmitt	1980–87	Chris Foster	1949–58	Max E.H. Hain	2003–12
John T. Devis	1967–76	James Foster	2007–14	William R.P. Hain	1947–56
Bryan Diamond	1946–54	Jeremy I. Fowler	1952–62	Glen Hales	1949–55
Sam Dillon	2009–	Timothy J. Fowler	1946–56	Peter Hall	1941–45
Richard Dingle	1963–74	Joshua Fox	2008–	Charles Hamilton	2006–13
Calum Distin	2007–	Scott Francis	2010–	Vaughan Hamilton	2011–
Luke Distin	2009–	Simon Francis	2008–	Jaeyong Danny Han	2008–
Caroline Dixon	WS Staff 1992–	Nigel Freeman	1973–80	Mark Hancock	1991–96
Freddie Dixon	1996–07	Todd Freeman	2004–	Roland Hancock	1969–78
Guy Dixon	2013–	Gervald and Kathryn Frykman		Lau Lap Hang	2011–15
Roy Dixon	1973–81		WS Staff 1981–	Don Hanson	1945–53
G. Dolphin	2011–	Aaron Ching Hei Fung	2012–	Jake Harding	2013–
Tom Donaldson	2012–	SamAnthony Gaballa	2012–	D.A. Harris	1974–85
D.N. Doorbar	1968–72	Christopher Galyer	1972–81	N.G. Harris	1952–59
Anne Douglas	WS Staff 2008–	Captain David Gardner	1950–54	R.D. Harris	1976–87
Carrie Dowding	2002–12	Martin Garrett	1965–72	Henry Harrison	2006–
Peter Dowler	1948–55	Lawrence Gartshore	2012–	Moses Harrison	2006–
Max Downton	2008–	Francis Gaymond	1997–08	Matthew Harry	2004–11
Connor Doyle	2013–	Oliver Gaymond	1992–03	Dr Tim Harry	1963–73
Oliver Doyle	2013–	Elizabeth Gemmell	WS Staff 2006–	Alastair S. Harryman	2007–14
Joe Dunstan	1946–54	Edward Gillespie	2000–07	Olivia Hartwell	WS Staff 2009–
John Dutton	1965–73	Gus Gillespie	2003–	Sam Hatherly	2010–
Clive Edwards	1959–66	Harry Gillespie	2000–09	Louis Hawking	2004–
Glyn J.B. Edwards	1986–89	George Glennon	2005–12	Joseph J.D. Hawkins	2010–
John Eld	1956–67	Marcus Glennon	2009–	Patrick Haynes	2006–13
Grant Elliott	1972–82	Samuel P.W. Gooch	2008–	Charles Heaton	1969–80
James Elliott	2008–	Stephen Gough	1967–74	Mark Anthony Heaton	2000–07
Callum Ellis	2007–14	Abhimanyu Gowda	2010–13	David Hewitt	1941–46
Joshua Emery	2005–	Jonah Richard Graham	2010–	Martin Hewitt	1953–63
Thomas Emery	2005–12	Kyriakos Grammatopoulos	2006–	Martin Hewitt	1968–75
James Eslick	2012–	Adam Gray	2010–	Sebastian Higgins	2005–
Ed Evans	2007–14	Peter Gray	1943–49	Christopher Hill	1973–80
Nicholas Evans	1982–85	Colin Green	1980–90	Tony Hill	1942–48
William Evans	1989–97	Harry Greenway	1946–53	Robbie J. Hoare	2005–12

Thomas H. Hoare	2003–10
J.R. 'Ced' Holbrook	1955–62
David P. Holdback	1986–95
Jonathan A. Holdback	1984–89
Philip Holding	1972–79
Robert Holl-Allen (formerly Allen)
	1946–53
Andrew Holley	1970–80
Oliver Jack Hood	2012–
Anthony Hooker	1994–00
Jonathan Hooker	1996–04
Samuel Hooker	2001–09
Steven Hooper	2001–12
George Hopkins	2005–
William Hopkins	2001–12
G.T. Horn	1940–44
Tom Hornby	2012–
David R. Horne	1967–74
James Houlder	1989–96
Robert Howard	1997–08
Charles Huggins	2007–
Alex Hughes	WS Staff 1968–95
Andrew Hughes	1981–89
Gabriel G. Humphreys	2009–
Ray Hung	1987–94
Alex F. Hunt	2005–09
Harry G. Hunt	2010–
Thomas G. Hunt	2006–13
Ken S.L. Hutchinson	1933–41
John Gregory Hyams	1971–76
Alexander Hyde	2008–
Norman Hyde	1956–63
John Ingram	1950–56
Angela Ireland	
Ben J. Irwin	2006–13
Daniel J. Irwin	2004–11
Adam N.A. Jackson	2007–
Andrew Jackson	1988–99
O.G. James	1993–03
Harry Jenkins	2010–
Guy Jessett	2001–12
Edward Jobburn	2011–
Jack Jobling	2003–14
Christopher Ian Johnson	2006–13
Jamie Johnson	2008–14

Laurence Johnson	2005–14	A.K.C. Lau	1976–81	George Eames Matthews	2013–	Daniel Oates	2001–12
Nicholas Ian Johnson	2009–	Max Lawley	2008–	Jack Matthews	1948–53	Peter C. Ogden	1953–65
Terry Johnson	1950–60	Thomas Lawley	2009–	Rohith Mattu	2007–	Adam Oliver	2006–
Thomas E.K. Johnston-Smith	2007–14	William Lawley	2009–	Samuel Maunder	2012–	Daniel J. Oliver	2005–12
Toby C.N. Johnston-Smith	2008–	Oliver Lawrence	2012–	Daniel May	2013–	Max Owen	2010–
Julian Johnston	1964–67	Frank Lawson	1943–48	Michael May	1963–68	Matt Paden	2009–
Peter H.R. Johnston	1948–55	L.K.R. Lax	1947–54	Thomas Maycock	2008–	Alastair Page	1965–71
Ethan Jones	2008–	Hugo Layzell	2012–	D.E. Mayman	1938–44	Steve Paget	1963–68
George Jones	2008–	Oliver Layzell	2010–	Ralph G. Mazdon	1944–47	Joanna Painter	2003–
Henry James Charles Jones	2013–	Kristian Leask	2013–	David McCuaig	1946–53	Ian M. Painton	1941–47
Jonathan H.S. Jones	1957–64	Jimin Lee	2012–	John McCulloch	1979–86	Jack Panting	2007–14
Kieran Jones	2008–	Jack Leggatt	2002–13	Barney McElholm	2001–14	J.F.V. Pare	1945–53
Owen Jones	2008–	Jonathan Lelliott	1989–00	Tom McElholm	2001–14	Zac Parker	2012–
R.P.S. Jones	1941–46	Richard Lelliott	2000–11	Mr S. McGarr and Ms E. Bethel		David A. Parsons	1949–55
Sam Jones	1998–05	Thomas Lester	2012–	Edward McGovern	2003–	James Parsons	2007–14
Samuel Jones	2008–	Charles Z.C. Liang	2013–	Henry McGovern	2003–	Tom Parsons	2005–12
Stephen Jones	1963–74	Nick Liddell	1982–87	William McGovern	2003–	Peter Pauwels	1947–56
Hamish Lee Jordan	2013–	James Lockwood	2011–	Tom McKay	1993–98	David J. Payne	1956–65
Pradeep Kachhala	1993–99	Peter Lomas	1962–66	Chris McNee	1992–	Peter F. Payne	1936–40
Gavin Lake Kagan	1983–90	Jake Lota	2008–	James McSharry	2010–	W. Stuart Peacock	1963–75
Thomas A.V. Karnik	2005–	Loui James Loughran	2011–	Andrew Mead	1979–86	Simon M. Peall	2013–
Nigel Kay	1957–68	Mark Love	1960–71	Ravi Mehta	2011–	Ross Pearman	2009–
James Keay	2011–	J.C. Loynton	1961–68	Vijay Mehta	2011–	Richard Pemberton	1969–74
Nicholas Keegan		Alessandro Luciano	2003–14	Jonathan Meredith	1953–63	Joseph Perkins	2010–
Finn Kelly	2009–	Robert Luker	1949–59	Adam Merrell	2004–	Perry Family	2006–
Roger M. Kelly	1954–60	Donald Edward MacDonald	2013–	Daniel Merrell	2003–13	Rajan Phakey	2010–
Thomas Kelly	2011–	James Macpherson	1991–96	Alexander Meyrick	2012–	Andrew Phillips	2001–12
Derek Kendall	1951–59	Geoffrey Malins	1939–44	Greg Michael	1979–86	Kiron Thomas Phillips	2006–12
Dr Geoff Kerrison	1960–67	Maxwell Arthur Jack Manley	2012–	Robert Milburn	1964–75	Richard J. Phillips	2004–
Simon Kershaw	1970–77	Gregory A.D. Mann	1998–05	Henry Miles	2008–	Zanesh Joseph Phillips	2008–13
M.J. Kettell	1943–50	Harry Manship	2010–	David B. Millard	1946–55	James Peter George Pigden	2011–
Rajan Khosla	1985–94	Samuel Manship	2010–	Nicky Miller	2008–	James Pincott	2005–
Oliver Kilsby	2012–	Alan M. Marchant	1940–46	Zakary Milstein	2012–	James Plumb	1993–98
Jake Kilshaw	2010–	Daniel H. Marcus	2000–13	Elliot L.T. Mintz	2001–08	Max Plumb	2010–
Giles Edward King	2013–	David Marguerie	2005–	Patrick Moren	1944–47	Cameron Podmore	2007–
Daniel Kingman	2010–	Simon W. Marrison	1972–83	John Morley	1993–98	Stuart Podmore	1975–82
Daniel Kirby	2007–14	Jamie Marsh	2011–	Daniel Morris	2009–	Michael J. Poultney	1962–69
Gerry Knight	1946–51	Ben Marshall	1995–06	Nicholas Moss	2008–	Samuel Powell	1970–79
James Knight	2013–	Chris Marshall	2005–13	Louis Moss-Lawton	2007–	Angus Preston	2008–
Jordan Knight	2007–14	Keith Marshall	WS Staff 1992–	James Nash	2011–	Hamish Preston	2008–12
Harlan Kwok	2011–	Killian Marshall	2007–14	Mark Naylor	1961–72	Laurence David Price	1961–72
Benjamin Lambert	2009–	Carl Martin	2008–	Paul Nealon	1990–95	Jonathan D.S. Prosser	2012–14
G.J. Lane	WS Staff 1967–93	Reeve Martin	1963–72	Alex Ng	2013–	Chris Purvis	1980–87
Edwin Langdale	1945–52	John B. Mason	1947–50	Sam O'Connell	2008–	Geoff Raine	1953–59
James Langley	2006–	Cameron Massey	2012–	Milan P. Oakland	2011–	Paul Ramage	1948–59

Malcolm J. Randle	1941–46	Norman and Eunice Shorthose	1970–83	Calum Tam	2011–	Julien Wan	2011–

Malcolm J. Randle — 1941–46
Alfie Ratcliffe — 2009–
Harry Ratcliffe — 2012–
Max William Rawson — 2008–
Glyn Rayment — 1997–04
Gary Reader — 1975–82
Owen Redfern — 1950–56
George W. Revill — 1949–54
Gerard D.M. Rhodes — 2002–13
Christian Richards — 2008–
S.J. Richardson — 2000–07
Benjamin Riddle — 1998–05
Matthew Riley — 2004–
Oscar M. Roberts — 2012–
H.B. Robinson — 1930–38
Luke Robinson — 2009–
N.J. Robinson — 1955–66
Alexander Rogers — 2006–
Jonathan Rogers — 2003–14
Mark Rogers — 1975–82
Matthew Rogers — 2008–
William Rogers — 2008–
Thomas G. Romano — 2012–
Leonard Rose — 1946–52
Phillip Rothwell — 1994–01
Andrew Rowe — 1972–83
John Rowe — 1977–84
Barry Sadler — 1947–52
Nilay Sah — 2009–13
Jerome Saint — 1950–53
James Samwell — 1992–99
Jamie Sanghera — 2010–
Alwyn Saul — 1941–48
Andrew Sawyer — 1952–64
Matthias Schleifenbaum — 1992–93
David Scott — 1975–83
Paras Sehmar — 2008–15
Rahul Sehmar — 2005–12
Oliver Sengupta — 2012–
Godfrey Harwood Sewell — 1949–54
John A. Sheffield — 1953–60
Roy Sheridan — 1963–70
Sebastian Shields — 2004–
James Shillcock — 2004–
Christopher Short — 2008–

Norman and Eunice Shorthose — 1970–83
Ian Perry Choong-Wong Simester — 2006–13
Adam Simmons — 2000–11
Oliver Simpson — 2012–
Gurdev Singh — 2004–
Harnek Singh — 2004–
Edd Slack — 2008–
Michael Slade — 1978–87
Christopher Smith — 2004–11
David Smith — 1972–79
George Smith — 2001–13
Jonathan T. Smith — 1990–97
Luke Smith — 2008–11
Mike Smith — 1946–53
R.H. Smith — 1943–53
Edward Snook — 2008–
Thomas Spackman — 2001–08
William Spackman — 2003–10
Harry Spalding — 2013–
Dan Sparks — 1984–91
Tim Spencer — 1957–65
Luke Spill — 2004–14
Joe Spinney — 2008–
Benjamin Spoor — 2013–
J. Harry Stephenson — 1994–05
The Revd Andrew Stevens — 1955–63
David Bennett Stevens — 1968–74
Harvey Robert Stevens — 2007–
Peter W. Stevens — 1952–59
Jonathan Hitchman Stone — 1996–03
Charles G. Stoney — 1948–58
Samuel Storey — 1997–04
Charles T.F. Streeten — 2002–07
Henry T.F. Streeten — 2004–11
Michael Streets — 2009–
Henry Stride — 2009–
William Stride — 2009–
Alan Sturley — 1943–49
Sachin Sudhakaran — 2010–
David R. Summers — 1955–67
Andrew Suswain — 1966–73
Matthew Swift — 2010–
Richard Sykes — 1954–64
Jake Sylvester — 2012–

Calum Tam — 2011–
William Tanner — 2010–
Daniel Taylor — 2009–
Jamie Taylor — 2001–12
John Vincent (Spud) Taylor — 1952–58
Jamie Thomas — 2005–12
Sandeep Thomas — 2004–11
Noah Thorne — 2007–14
Jack Thornton — 1951–58
Ralph H. Thornton — WS Staff 1948–89
David Tickner — 1962–69
Clive Timms — 1957–64
Chris Todd — 1998–03
Theo Todd — 2011–
David Tolley — 1951–61
Adrian G.J. Toutoungi — 1981–91
Justin Tsui — 2012–14
Nigel Tubb — 1969–77
Stephen Tubb — 1971–82
Sam Tugwood — 2008–
Chris Tunbridge — 2005–12
Janet Turner — WS Staff 1989–
Peter Robert Turner — 1956–63
Simon Turner — 1968–73
Thomas Robert Turner — 1921–26
Cian Tyler — 2013–
Stelios Tzirki — 2007–14
Hardev Uppal — 2007–14
George Vahey — 2013–
John G. Varnish — 1950–60
Jonathan Varnish — 2010–
Thomas Varnish — 2010–
Fraser Venn — 2012–
George Vetch — 2004–14
Roger Sebastian Vidal — 2012–
Edward Vining — 2002–10
Jonathan Vining — 2011–
Ferdinand Leo von Holstein — 2002–13
Johnny R. von Holstein — 2006–
Ray Walder — 1953–60
Jamie Walker — 2006–
Chris Walsh — 2005–12
Stephen Walsh — 2007–14
D.H. Walter — 1950–55
S.M. Walter — 1982–89
Charles and Diana Wan

Julien Wan — 2011–
Murray M. Wankling — 2007–14
Montague John Ward — 1943–49
Nick Waterworth — 1969–77
Dr Charles Watmough — WS Staff 1983–04
Cameron Watson — 2011–
Harry Watts — 2010–
Oliver H. Webb — 1988–95
Patrick Wegerdt — 1977–88
Daniel Weir — 2002–12
Geoffrey Weir — 1959–65
Sam Weir — 2002–12
C.M. West — 1945–55
John Whick — 1990–97
Anthony P. White — 1952–58
Charlie White — 2000–04
Bill Whitfield — 1947–54
Nicholas Whiting — 1956–63
Richard Whiting — 1958–69
G. Wilkes — 2012–
David Wilkinson — 1958–66
Aaron Williams — 2009–
Albert Williams — 2009–
Frederick Williams — 2005–
James Williams — 2007–
James Williams — 1987–00
Kenneth J. Wills — 1949–56
Michael Colin Willson — 1948–57
David Wilson — 1973–80
Peter Wilson — 1979–85
Robert McNeil Wilson — 1967–74
Michael Wolverson — 2008–
Jasper Wong — 2012–
Harry Woodhead — 2012–
Matthew Woodhouse — 1981–92
F.J. (John) Woodward — 1945–53
Richard Worrall — 1997–03
Alan P. Wright — 1945–56
Roger J. Wyatt — 1950–58
John A. Yarwood — 1947–53
David Yates — 2008–
Richard Yates — 2010–
Ryan Yeung — 2012–14
Eugene Yick — 2005–
Barry Young — WS Staff 1949–85

PICTURE CREDITS

The majority of the contemporary photographs used in this book were taken by Alan Davidson (www. stills-photography.co.uk).

Peter O'Grady, Deputy Head (Academic), has taken on the role of official school photographer over the years, and many of his photographs are included in this volume as well.

We are grateful in addition to the *Birmingham Post and Mail*, *Coventry Evening Telegraph*, *Leamington Spa Courier Series* and Gillman & Soame, all of whom have kindly agreed for us to reproduce their photos.

We also wish to thank: C. Birt (1940 p.23, skating p.75, camp p.76), D. Clarke (*Jesus Christ Superstar* p.63 bottom), J. Clift (charity walk p.85), T. Dalton (p.120), S. Dee (jazz p.87), J. Dunstan (p.102), M. Eaves (cross country p.53), W. Grimes (*Treasure Island* p.45), R. Hancox (1934–5 rugby p.50), N. Harris (p.40), John (Tan) Hooper (1940s p.116), S. Jennings (1923 cubicles, p.48), P. Johnston (p.40), Lord Leycester Hospital (p.11), Mrs Ros Partridge (p.24), Photo-Reportage Ltd, D. Shield (Adventurous Training p.122), The Revd Andrew Stevens (p.128), R.H. Thornton (Chapel p.16, Chapel Choir p.66), R. Titchen (bridge p.110), R. Usherwood (Harvest Festival p.37, Christmas p.68), Warwick County Record Office (Speede map p.10), A. Westwood (P. Whitlam p.25), R. Wilmut (1961 assembly p.42, orchestra p.47, Chapel Quad p.76)

… and many others who have donated their photos.

*Deputy Head (and school photographer)
Peter O'Grady, in action at the Design
and Technology Crest Awards 2013,
photographed by Alan Davidson.*

1898-H.D.S.KEIGHLEY, passed into Sandhurst.

1899-F.DAVIS, Open Mathematical Scholarship.Corpus Christi College, Cambridge.

1899-K.W.BARLEE, Trinity College. Dublin. 3rd Classical Scholarship.

1899-G.B.STRATTON, Eastern Cadetship.

1899-G.G.SUMNER, Whitworth Exhibition.

1899-H.J.NORMAN-DAVIS, passed into Sandhurst.

1900-W.B.BAKER, passed 26th into Sandhurst.

1900-E.L.GERRARD, passed into Sandhurst.

1900-W.T.SOUTHORN, 2nd Class. Classical Moderations.

1900-L.F.CASS. 3rd Class. Natural Science Tripos. Pt. I.

1900-F.DAVIS, Foundation Scholarship. Corpus Christi College, Cambridge.

1900-K.W.BARLEE, passed 41st for the Indian Civil Service.